Centre Georges Pompidou Paris

Text by
Jean Poderos

D0150336

≋ Centre
Pompidou

Prestel

Munich · Berlin · London · New York

**Georges Pompidou National Centre
of Art and Culture**

Jean-Jacques Aillagon *President*
Bruno Maquart *Director*
Alfred Pacquement *Director of the MNAM*
Dominique Païni *Director of the DDC*
Gérald Grunberg *Director of the BPI*
Bernard Stiegler *Director of IRCAM*
Jean-Pierre Marcie-Rivière *Chairman of the
       Centre Pompidou's development association*
François Trèves *Chairman of the Amis du Musée*

The concept of this guide was developed
by the Publishing Department of the Centre
Pompidou, Paris

Emmanuel Fessy *Director*
Philippe Bidaine *Deputy director*
Françoise Bertaux *Project manager*
Benoît Collier *Commercial manager*
Mathias Battestini, Claudine Guillon
       Rights and contracts

Jean Poderos *Author*
Françoise Savatier *Proofreader*

The publishers thank everyone who has
kindly assisted in the realisation of this work.

at MNAM-CCI
conservation: Isabelle Monod-Fontaine,
Jean-Paul Ameline, Agnès de La Beaumelle,
Jean-Michel Bouhours, Sophie Duplaix,
Alison Gingeras, Frédéric Migayrou,
Nadine Pouillon, Alain Sayag, Jonas Storsve,
Christine Van Assche
with the help of: Monica Baillon, Lucia
Daniel, Danièle Janton, Patrick Palaquer,
Étienne Sandrin, Sylvie Chabot
documentation of the collection: Didier
Schulmann, Évelyne Pomey, Malika Noui
Museum documentation: Agnès de Bretagne,
Christine Sorin, Brigitte Vincens

at the BPI Colette Timsit
at IRCAM Sophie Manceau de Lafitte
at the DAEP Josée Chapelle, Marie-Jo
       Nguyen-Poisson
at the DDC François Nemer
at the audio-visual service Guy Carrard
and at the Publishing Department Martial
       Lhuillery

English edition
ISBN 3-7913-2708-9

Printed in Germany

Prestel Verlag
Mandlstrasse 26
80802 Munich
Tel. +49 (89) 38 17 09-0, Fax 38 17 09-35
www.prestel.com

© Éditions du Centre Pompidou, Paris /
Prestel Verlag, Munich · Berlin · London ·
New York, 2002

Translated from the French by
Paul Aston, London
Copy-edited by Danko Szabó, Munich
Typography, Design and Production by
Heinz Ross, Obergries (heinzross@t-online.de)
Origination by Reproline GmbH, Munich
Printing and binding by Passavia GmbH, Passau

Contents

Foreword

Since it was opened in 1977, the Georges Pompidou National Centre of Art and Culture has realised an ambition to unite in one place the different forms and practices of contemporary culture and creation. These include the visual arts, represented both by the prestigious collections of the National Museum of Modern Art/Industrial Design Centre and a substantial programme of temporary exhibitions; the books, the press and new technologies at the Public Reference Library (BPI); music, in the works and events put on by the IRCAM (Institut de recherche et de co-ordination acoustique/musique); and finally, film, theatre, dance and new forms of live performance, which are particularly welcome.

Cutting across all these disciplines and contrasting them with current trends, the Centre is also an ongoing forum for debate and intellectual exchange.

It is the living dynamism and originality of the whole project that accounts for its continued success. The Centre now attracts over six million visitors a year, making it – along with the Louvre – the most visited cultural institution in France and, therefore, undoubtedly one of the most popular in Europe, and indeed the world.

With a public of this size and diversity, we were duty bound to come up with a publication that presents the richness of the Centre's collections and range of its activities, written in the languages spoken in every continent. Such a work would also help our visitors to find their way quickly and easily around the seven levels and 90,000 m² of building designed by architects Renzo Piano and Richard Rogers.

That, then, is the object of the present guide, which is available in French, English, Italian, German, Spanish and Japanese. The first edition coincides with the 25th anniversary of the Centre Georges Pompidou , following its recent renovation and reorganisation. The reader will find it not only a delightful prelude to a wholly successful and properly enjoyed visit but also a reliable introduction to 20th-century art and contemporary work. What is involved here is a comfortable stroll through the collections of the National Museum of Modern Art, taking a detailed look at 150 of the masterpieces.

So you need to find room for this book in your baggage as well as on your bookshelves. Just now, though, all you need to do is open it and let it show you round. Welcome to the Centre Georges Pompidou!

JEAN-JACQUES AILLAGON
Chairman, Centre Pompidou

The Centre Pompidou, National Centre of Art and Culture
Art and Culture for Everyone

✦ Entrance via Place Georges-Pompidou,
75004 Paris, 100 yards [2 minutes'
walk] from Boulevard Sébastopol

The Centre Pompidou already
has a long history. It was first
mooted more than 20 years ago,
in 1969, when the French president,
Georges Pompidou, dreamed
of Paris having a 'cultural centre
that was both a museum and
a creative centre, where the visual
arts would rub shoulders with
music, film, books and audio-visual
studies' – but also a people's place,
where everyone would be able
to access all culture and all forms
of art as freely as possible.

The building

It was an ambitious project, har-
bouring within it the spirit of Babel.

Footbridge on the 6th floor

Georges Pompidou (1911-1974)

Educated at the École normale supérieure (*grand école* for teacher training), gaining an arts *agrégation* (higher-level teacher qualification) and diploma in Science and Politics.

Taught in Marseilles and then Paris. Following the Liberation, entered politics and, as a close associate of General de Gaulle, became his prime minister in 1962, remaining in this post until 1968. After de Gaulle's resignation, he was elected President of the Republic in 1969.

A highly cultured man and collector of contemporary art, he was also the author of an anthology of French poetry, which has now become a classic.

From the moment he became president, he made it clear that he intended to open a National Centre of Art and Culture that was both multidisciplinary and non-elitist. His premature death in office in 1974 meant he never saw his dream completed.

Following her husband's example, his widow, Madame Claude Pompidou, staunchly and consistently championed the Centre, its values and its objectives.

The building to be erected in the historic heart of the capital would need to respond to multi-disciplinary requirements, while providing easy circulation and maximum openness in the exhibition areas. Among the 681 projects considered by the jury of the international competition set up for the occasion, it was the one submitted by two young architects, the Italian Renzo Piano and Briton Richard Rogers, that carried the day on 15 July 1971. Their scheme was selected particularly for the extent to which it accorded with the multi-disciplinary requirement for the Centre, the quality it brought to the surrounding area, the way it gathered the various activities together within a single volume, and the flexibility of use it offered.

The dream gave birth to an architectural revolution. Influenced by the Archigram group, who in the 1960s put forward a libertarian and highly inventive approach to architecture that never made reality, Piano and Rogers proposed creating a machine whose architectural details are emblematic of this new approach. The structural elements and the circulation system within it, such as the huge snaking flight of escalators, are pushed outside, leaving the whole interior as space for activities. The latter, organised into wide decks of 7,500 m² each, can be completely reorganised as the Centre's needs evolve. The transparency of the main façade means that what is going on inside can be seen from the huge plaza that the two architects decided to create along the west front, the building occupying only one of the 7,500 m² of land that the State acquired on the Beaubourg plateau. The sole exception was IRCAM, the institute for musical and acoustical research, which for technical reasons was installed in Place Igor Stravinsky, below the area where Jean Tinguely and Niki de Saint-Phalle's fountain now stands.

An anti-monument

A liner, a city within a city, a tubular machine or a gasworks – the Pompidou Centre has been the subject of fulsome compliments and all kinds of gibes. Even if, as an example of modernity, it still upsets some, it is nonetheless now

The Centre in figures

- The Pompidou Centre was opened on 31 January 1977
- Surface area of the building c. 90,000 m² (nearly 1 million sq. ft)
- Volume: 430,000 m³ (over 15 million cu. ft)
- Eight storeys, five of them as super-structure
- 166 m (545 ft) long, 42 m (138 ft) high, 60 m (197 ft) wide
- The steel frame of the building is built of girders 45 m (148 ft) long and 3 m (nearly 10 ft) high.
- The storeys are 7 m (23 ft) high below the ceiling, with a girder every 12 m (39 ft) set 4 m (12 ft) above floor level.
- The interior areas are huge decks with an area of 7,500 m² (81,000 sq. ft).
- The Centre reopened on 1 January 2000 after 27 months of works, during which time it was virtually completely closed.
- 70,000 m² (765,000 sq. ft.) were renovated, while 8,000 m² (86,400 sq. ft.) of supplementary space were freed up after the offices were moved outside the building.

Colours at the Centre

On the east front, facing Rue du Renard, the servicing shafts are rendered in different colours to show their function:
- blue for air ducts
- green for the pipework for liquids
- yellow for electrical shafts
- red for people movement (lifts, etc.)

The architects of the renovation

'A building that would be not a monument but a celebration, a large urban plaything.'

Renzo Piano, architect

Renzo Piano, one of the two original architects of the Centre, and Jean-François Bodin, an architect already well-known for his work at numerous French museums, were appointed to carry out the renovation. Dominique Jakob and Brendan McFarlane designed the new restaurant on the 6th floor and its spectacular interior architecture of metal shells.

The gerberettes

On each level of the structure, enormous steel vertebrae seem to come straight from marine engineering, reinforcing the idea of the Centre being a ship.
Called 'gerberettes' (after their inventor, Gerber), these components, aligned on an axis, are braced at the end by tie-rods anchored in the ground, the other extremity being the support on which the girder sits. The vertical posts are supplied with a water system which automatically sprinkles the suspension components in the event of fire.

View of the 6th floor west terrace. In the foreground is Max Ernst's The Large Tortoise and the Large Frog, *1967-1994*

View of the east front

The outside escalator

The Centre under construction, 1974

Part of the metal framework

A deck being renovated, 1999

Further reading

- *Centre Pompidou, l'esprit du lieu*, by Philippe Bidaine, co-published by Centre Pompidou/Scala, 2001, € 5,34
The architecture of the Pompidou Centre and the history of its establishment in one of the oldest quarters in Paris.

- *Le Centre Georges Pompidou, Piano – Rogers*, Élizabeth Amzallag-Augé et Sophie Curtil, published by Centre Pompidou, 1996, French and English, (€ 12,20) and Japanese, (€ 12,96)
A playful discovery – for children – of the Pompidou Centre

- *Le Centre Georges Pompidou*, film by Richard Copans, coproduced by Centre Pompidou/Les Films d'ici/La Sept-Arte, 2000, € 15,09
Analyses the various phases of construction of the Pompidou Centre with the aid of reconstructed building models.

- *Métro Rambuteau*, by Marc Petitjean, co-published by Centre Pompidou/Hazan, 1997, € 14,48
Photographic history of the radical transformation of Paris's historical Quartier de l'Horloge for the construction of the Pompidou Centre.

- *Renzo Piano, architecte au long cours*, film by Marc Petitjean, coproduction by Centre Pompidou/Mirage illimité/Grand Canal, 2000, € 21,19
A portrait of Renzo Piano via four major building projects.

- *Georges Pompidou, homme de culture*, Philippe Tétart, 1995, € 21,34
Text of the symposium: Georges Pompidou, homme de culture.

Extramural activities

The Centre acts as a channel for art far beyond its own walls, organising exhibitions and performances both in the regions and abroad. These are major events first put on at the Centre that subsequently go on tour, or else are specifically created for abroad, a recent example being 'Parade,' an exhibition staged in Brazil in 2001 illustrating the National Museum of Modern Art's collections.

accepted above all as one of the emblematic monuments of Paris. And it is no doubt in this apparent contradiction that the Centre is seen as a model – a place of both conservation and creation. Its architects conceived it as an anti-monument, a machine for disorder, unfinished and in constant mutation, and yet still a building that, as Georges Pompidou reminded Piano and Rogers, would last four or five centuries.

Success

The Centre rapidly became successful beyond all expectations. Instead of 5,000 visitors a day, the average quickly reached 22,000, or more than seven million admissions a year. It became Paris's most visited monument, outclassing even Nôtre-Dame. This triumph of popularity goes hand in hand with that of the Library, whose very substantial encyclopaedic open-access collection has attracted not only all the students from the Paris area but also members of the public less used to visiting such places. This success can be attributed equally to certain exhibitions that have become legendary (Paris-Berlin, 1978, Dalí, 1979-80, Matisse, 1992, Brancusi, 1995, Le Temps, vite, 2000) and the National Museum of Modern Art's own collection, one of the finest in the world. The debates, meetings and dance performances organised nowadays by the Department of Cultural Development (DDC) are attracting a new public to the Centre that is rarely seen at its other activities.

Annual pass

An annual season ticket giving the right to priority access via Place Georges-Pompidou, with free entry to the Museum, exhibitions and cinemas (except during festivals) at any time, at reduced rates for performances and numerous other benefits. See 'Annual Pass' in *From A to Z (p. 154)*.

Less well-known, but vital for the multi-disciplinary approach of the Centre, is IRCAM, which has at the same time managed to convince the musical world of the exclusivity of its studies and quality of its achievements.

Renewal

Twenty years have passed. The difficulties and unknown factors inherent in the life of a machine such as this could never mar the successes. However, it became clear that the Centre was showing its age and in need of renovation.

Work began in October 1997, requiring the complete closure of the Centre, and was basically complete by January 2000. Opportunity was taken to make improvements and enlargements, the most important of which concerned the Museum and the Library. The National Museum of Modern Art/Industrial Design Centre (MNAM-CCI), which now occupies two entire floors of the building, has a display from its contemporary collections on Level 4 and a selection of the modern art collections on Level 5. The Public Reference Library (BPI), which has its own entrance in the Forum, has had its floor space and sources of information extended to provide an improved response to the challenge of the new media.

Since the Centre re-opened, its popularity has been maintained, a tremendous vote of confidence by the public, which has thus indicated its profound attachment and continued adherence to the place and its spirit.

[i]

For opening hours, telephone enquiries, tickets and charges, please refer to the relevant headings in *From A to Z (pp. 154ff.)*.

Services

- Enquiries and information
  – General information desk – Forum, Level 0
  – Museum information – Level 4
- Ticket machines (only full-rate tickets, payment by credit card) – Forum, Level 0.
- Cloakroom, toilets, post office, cash machines, telephones – Forum, Level 0.
- Annual pass area – Forum, Level 0.
- Bookshops – Levels 0, 4 and 6.
- Design boutique – Forum, Level 1.
- Mezzanine café – Forum, Level 1.
- Cafeteria kiosk – Library, Level 2.
- Georges Restaurant, with panoramic terrace – Level 6. Reservations on 01-44 78 47 99 (access from outside via Place Georges-Pompidou, separate lift).
- Parking – access via underground entrance from Les Halles or Rue Beaubourg (corner of Rue Rambuteau).

🖳 www.centrepompidou.fr

Set up in 1995, the Pompidou Centre website was completely redesigned while renovation works were going on. This is the place to visit for more details.

- The **Agenda** covers current news about the Centre's programmes and activities.
- **Évenements** (Events) gives information about all the specific activities at the Centre.
- **Expositions** contains summaries of the various exhibitions, with images.
- The **Musée** (Museum) section deals with the displays and new acquisitions and provides a chronicle of 20th-century art for educational purposes.
- **Documentation** is intended for research, and includes catalogues, archives etc.
- **Éditions** contains a catalogue of publications in French by the publications department.
- The **BPI** and **Ircam** sites can also be accessed from here. See *Websites* in *From A to Z (p. 158)*.

Signage

Since it reopened, the Centre has had a new corporate design and signage to guide visitors, developed by the studio of Ruedi Baur Associates as project managers and based on the legendary typewriter characters of Jean Widmer.

The large signs, echoing the Centre's colour scheme, repeat simple words, like carbon copies, to provide the same information in different languages. Evocative and with great visual presence, this signage is a potent and effective link between the architecture and the cultural programme.

The Stravinsky fountain, with works by Jean Tinguely and Niki de Saint-Phalle

Queuing to get into the Pompidou Centre

The activities of the Forum and exhibitions at the Centre
Things to do and see

✛ In the Forum, Levels 0, 1 and –1

You pass under the canopy to enter the Centre's Forum. The Forum is more than simply a place to take your bearings, because this is where you will find out how the Pompidou Centre works. Immediately ahead is a general enquiries and information desk. At the back, on the left, is the ticket office for the Museum, the exhibitions and shows. Turning further left, an escalator leads either to the flights of escalators up to the Museum on Level 4 or the exhibitions (Level 6), or alternatively, to the open-access Design boutique, the Library and cinema screen 1.

On the right, a large bookstore carries all the Centre's publications on sale and a wide selection of

An installation at the Crossroads of Creation in the Forum

end of this book, in the A to Z of Practical Information.)

Welcome, therefore, to the Pompidou Centre – a busy place where curiosity is always aroused by the apparent confusion of genres and the mixture of activities. Performances and live events, debates, meetings, films, temporary exhibitions and educational activities coincide, cross-fertilise, raise issues, intertwine …

The 'Crossroads of Creation' (Levels 0 and 1)

From the moment you enter, and all round the huge pit that opens on to Level –1, various bizarre, improbable, or at least unfamiliar, objects come into view, leaving you at first unsure whether you are in an exhibition or a shop. It is an intentional disorientation, an essential questioning process in the approach to the Crossroads of Creation. Regularly presented here are creations of contemporary design or objects produced by industrial design.

works on modern and contemporary visual arts. Another escalator leads to the South Gallery for exhibitions and the café on Level 1.

At the back, behind the enquiries desk, two staircases and two lifts take you to Levels 1 and –1. Level –1 is where most of the performances and live events and certain conferences take place. (The other facilities of the Forum are shown at the

Educational activities (Level 0)

One of the core features of the Pompidou Centre as a place open to all kinds of public is its educational role. Numerous activities are available to the interested public (whether specialist or uninitiated), young visitors, their families and teachers. Specific visits are available for disabled people.

The area for the youngest visitors is in the Forum: the Children's Gallery and Education Space are installed on the left, beneath the mezzanine floor.

The Gallery puts on two exhibitions a year for children, with various associated workshops. In the Education Space at the back, other workshops probe modern and contemporary art in greater depth. Thanks to 'From the studio to the Museum,' children can explore the world of the painter or sculptor, themselves producing coloured environments, giant frescoes or spatial installations; they subsequently go on to discover the works that inspired their own creations. 'Active visits to the Museum' enables children and their parents to approach works in the permanent collection through play activities and the senses: two educational packs – Blue, Yellow, Red and Matter for Sensation – provide an opportunity to discover paintings via the three primary colours, and sculptures through the different materials artists use.

For adults and students, the 'One Sunday, One Work' conferences are an occasion to select a work from the Museum's collections and to look at its history and analyse it, while the recently established Collège du Centre [Pompidou Centre College] investigates the history of 20th-century concepts, movements and artists through conferences based on topics associated with temporary exhibitions and the Museum's collections. Meetings with creative artists, workshops, series of visits and architectural walks also accompany the public in its exploration of the Pompidou Centre.

Finally, the Centre also has a role to play in artistic training. School groups – from infant schools to the sixth form – come on visits throughout the year. The Centre

Department of Cultural Development [DDC]

The DDC is based in the Centre Pompidou. It oversees all the performances, live events and spoken word, film and audio-visual activities. Like the Museum, it is an exhibition organiser. Its brief is to highlight the cultural, anthropological and sociological changes in our societies.

Performances and live events

Level –1
- Performances and live events occupy three rooms:
  – the Grand Salle [Large Hall] (440 seats, dance, theatre, music)
  – the Petite Salle [Small Hall] (160 seats, conferences)
  – Cinema Screen 2 (150 seats)
- The foyer is reserved for services (ticket machines, bar and cloakroom), but can also be used for cultural events and installations of works relating to the performance or event.

Level 1
Cinema Screen 1 (320 seats)

What an artist said

Choreographer Merce Cunningham:
"The Centre is full of surprises on all levels. The entente between public and arts, the plastic arts as well as performance arts, is a work of genius."

Educational and Public Policy Directorate (DAEP)

In its constant ambition to further access to today's art and culture for as many people as possible, the Centre has set up a special department to look after educational activities. The DAEP plans the activities of the Children's Gallery and the Educational Area, and oversees all other educational aspects, particularly in the Museum.

View of the Forum

Farewell show by Yves Saint Laurent, Pompidou Centre, 22 January 2002. (Photo: D.R.)

also organises training courses for teachers and staff of the education services, both internal and extra-mural.

Live events (Level –1)

One of the great innovations on the reopening of the Centre in 2000 was the renewal of the live event sphere of activities, the equivalent for the theatrical arts of the 'contemporary art' part of the Museum. Dance, theatre, electronic music, but also performances and fashion shows, are now integrated in the Centre's programmes. Besides great artistes such as Patti Smith or Steve Reich, the institution also caters for the young scene. It thus enables a wide public to become familiar with con-temporary live work. The live event organisers have also set up joint initiatives with other departments and welcome input from the visual arts and design, or musical creation from IRCAM, particularly during the Agora festival.

Spoken Reviews (Level –1)

A feature ever since the Centre opened in 1977, the Spoken Reviews are among its long-standing activi-ties. They take the form of themed discussions on different aspects of creation in relation to the visual and applied arts, philosophy and litera-ture, and take place throughout the year. Three times a year, special Reviews provide an opportunity, over three evenings, to cross discip-lines and modes of intervention. Finally, also three times a year, the Reviews take the form of inter-national symposia.

Social forums (Level –1)

Another regular feature is large forums attracting specialists from every country to debate major phe-nomena of our world. Overturning received ideas, they underline the links between artistic creation and social change. The subject matter is always linked to current cultural, audio-visual or new-media topics, or else is selected for its relevance to the Centre's programme of exhib-itions.

Films (Levels 1 and –1)

The Centre's film sessions are organised around extensive series which explore a particular topic, illustrate a temporary exhibition or present a film-maker or school (Hitchcock, Russian and Soviet films, etc.). Along with the retro-spective sessions, the programme of film activities also focuses on audio-visual creation involving the new media, especially the Internet.

Videodance (Level –1)

Dance is essentially an ephemeral art. How then do we show the work of Nijinsky or Loïe Fuller? How can we preserve the performances of Merce Cunningham or Pina Bausch? Videodance is an annual festival that offers the public a chance to view outstanding archive films and to explore choreographed creations specifically intended for video.

---

i

Address: Centre Pompidou, Place Georges-Pompidou, 75004 Paris.

For the Children's Programme, guided tours, conferences, group visits, informa-tion for the disabled, training and courses, please refer to the relevant headings in *From A to Z (pp. 154 ff.)*.

*An Active
Visit in the
Museum,
looking
at Xavier
Veilhan's* **Rhinoceros**

*Children's
workshop,
Soulages
series*

*Children's
workshop,
Giacometti
series*

Guided tour of the Museum

Entry to the Raymond Hains exhibition, 27 June-3 September 2001

The exhibitions

✦ On the mezzanine level, r. h. side of the Forum (Level 1), and on Level 6

Temporary exhibitions play a vital part in the life and success of the Centre. They are its way of keeping up with and commemorating artistic and cultural developments.

Apart from the major retrospectives of single artists, there have been notable themed exhibitions in the Museum's programme that have done much to promote the Centre's multi-disciplinary mission, bringing together three-dimensional works, architecture and design, not to mention film, multimedia and documentary resources. They include 'Paris-New York' (1977), 'The Earth's Magicians' (1989), 'In the Face of History' (1996) and, more recently, 'Time, Quickly!' (2000), 'The Pop Years' (2001) and 'Hitchcock and Art' (2001). Some of them have effectively been experimental laboratories, occasionally changing the way a viewer sees an exhibition. Examples are 'Immaterials' (1985), 'Formless' (1996), 'Imprints' (1997) and 'Sonic Process' (2002).

Yet others have provided visitors with an opportunity to get to grips with the fundamental issues of modern and contemporary creation. Among these are 'Malevich, Planities and Architectones' (1980), 'Gaetano Pesce, Time for Questions' (1996), 'Beyond Spectacle' (2001), 'Nan Goldin, Will o' the Wisp' (2001) and 'Paint me, Dear Painter' (2002). These titles represent only a tiny part of the hundreds of exhibitions put on at the Centre since 1977.

The different teams at the Centre regularly work together to draw up multiple sections of an exhibition. Whether it is IRCAM, Performances and Live Events and the Library can join in or stage complementary activities relating to the subject being presented. It is this multi-disciplinarity that makes the Centre Pompidou so different.

Top 10 exhibitions by visitor numbers

Dalí	1979/80	840,662
Matisse	1993	734,896
Bonnard	1984	488,093
Paris-Paris	1981	473,103
Vienna	1986	450,000
Brancusi	1995	431,764
Paris-Moscow	1979	425,013
Magritte	1979	386,313
Francis Bacon	1996	363,215
The Pop Years	2001	354,090

Further reading

Most exhibitions are accompanied by a catalogue (sometimes a book) providing further information on the subject. Such publications complement a visit to the exhibition. They are on sale in the Centre's bookshops and elsewhere in France and abroad. The catalogue of the Centre's publications department (Éditions du Centre Pompidou) contains 500 titles and can be sent on request (+33-[0]1-44 78 42 30) or consulted on the Centre's website, www.centrepompidou.fr.

ℹ️

• Opening hours
The exhibitions are open daily 11 am to 9 pm, except Tuesdays and 1 May.

⚠️

Last entry 8 pm.
The galleries close at 8.45 pm.

• Tickets and charges
Please refer to the relevant heading in *From A to Z (pp.154 ff.).*

• Guided tours
For guided tours, conferences, group visits, disabled visitors, please refer to these headings in *From A to Z (pp.154 ff.).*

• Audioguides in French, English and Italian are available for certain exhibitions. Available at the entrance to the exhibitions.

Reading, Seeing, Listening, Learning

✦ During the week, entry is via the Forum. Closed Tuesdays and 1 May. At weekends and on public holidays and when Vigipirate anti-terrorist measures are in force, entry is via Rue du Renard (other side of the Centre).

A unique library

The Public Reference Library [BPI] is unique in France. It is an encyclopaedic library open to readers free of charge and without registration. It contains 2,200 seated places, 8 ¾ miles of bookshelves and 400 computer terminals. The opportunities are vast: you can research a tricky subject or simply browse, listen to music, watch documentary films, read the whole world's press or watch foreign TV, study one of 125 languages available, freely roam the Internet or

The Library (BPI). General view of the reading room on Level 2

History

- 1967   Establishment of the Public Reference Library (BPI) to provide open-access multi-media collections
- 1976   The Library is set up by decree as a public national institution.
- 1977   The Centre opens. Inauguration of the Library comprising a news room in the Forum, which becomes immensely popular.
- 1978   International Documentary Film Festival launched. It has established a worldwide reputation.
- 1980   Exhibition of 'Maps and Diagrams of the Earth.'
- 1984   The librarians handle catalogue information directly on computer. Exhibition: 'The Kafka Century.'
- 1986   Reconstruction of the Café Viennois during the 'Vienna 1880-1938' exhibition.
- 1987   'Memories of the Future' exhibition.
- 1988   'The Ideal Library' exhibition – the 2,500 books every civilised man should know.
- 1989 The Library welcomes its 50 millionth reader.
- 1990   Bi-centenary exhibition – the 'Forum of the Revolution.'
- 1990   'Tele/visions of the World' exhibition.
- 1992   'Jorge Luis Borges' exhibition.
- 1994   'Walter Benjamin, Le Passant, La Trace' exhibition.
- 1997   BPI Library areas in the Centre closed and moved (until 1999) to interim accommodation in the Rue Brantôme.
- 1998   First Rendez-vous de l'édition (publishers' conference) with the support of the Syndicat national de l'édition
- 2000   Centre and Public Reference Library re-open following complete reorganisation by architect Jean-François Bodin.

go to one of 750 selected sites – and, of course, take down and read any book you like. The section for job hunters and the information about jobs and companies are equally in demand.

A unique role

As a national-level multimedia library open to all, the BPI has been a hit ever since the Centre opened.

The huge diversity of its resources, available in open access, is one of the essential factors of its popularity. It brings together, in fact, within an area under a hundred paces long, works of French and foreign literature – often in both the original language and French translation – medical manuals or art books. The visitor can choose to listen to a techno pop disc or church music, or consult a CD-ROM business directory or the official EU journal.

Likewise, the extended opening hours, following the example of the Centre, make for a wide utilization. In 2000, students (59%) were the most numerous, while employes (20%) generally used it after 6 p.m.

A variety of resources

In addition to the traditional major subject sections (on Levels 2 and 2) such as Literature, History and Geography or Science and Technology, the BPI has added four new areas enabling readers to make more efficient use of the resources. On Level 1, the Reference section specialises in aiding bibliographical research and providing detailed information. Readers can consult catalogues of other libraries here, or encyclopaedias and dictionaries, atlases or phone directories, or obtain practical information about life in the Paris area and job hunting, particularly on the Internet. With 2,500 periodicals, on-line press publications and 11 TV channels on 16 sets, the Press section provides information derived from every country in the world. The Self-Study section (120 places) is open to all, allowing everyone to learn new languages and the use of software in the way and at the speed he/she prefers, or to brush up on certain basic knowledge. The Video & Sound section houses the BPI's collection of recordings, comprising musical recordings and spoken

Art among the books

In 1969, opening the library of the Centre that would later bear his name, French president Georges Pompidou dreamt of a place that would attract thousands of readers who would at the same time be in contact with the arts. The Library's management wanted this contact to be direct, and hung some of the Museum's works within its walls. A huge painting therefore adorns the staircase and a work by Lawrence Weiner is installed at the entrance to the third floor.

Documentary films

Every spring, the Library organises its Documentary Film Festival, dedicated to documentaries by leading-edge contemporary film-makers. The festival has, over the years, established a reputation both at home and abroad and thus helped many documentary film-makers to gain international recognition.

Congestion at the Library

The long line to get into the Library is well-known, and can sometimes involve a wait of up to two hours.
The best way to beat the line is to avoid weekends and go in any case after 6 p.m. Note that Friday is the quietest day of the week.

Library activities

- Familiarisation sessions with research tools.
- Series of meetings, debates, reading workshops.
- Literary walks taking in parts of Paris that have inspired writers.
- International symposia on subjects relating to written matter and books.
- Film screenings every Wednesday, showing a documentary at 12.30 and 8 pm and a children's film at 2.30 pm.

⚠

Information about programmes on 01-44 78 44 49 or www.bpi.fr.

Self-study section

The Public Reference Library in figures

- 10,000 m² (108,000 sq. ft.)
- Three levels
- 8 ¾ miles (14 km) of shelves
- 2,200 seated places
- Open 62 hours a week
- Five booths equipped for the blind and partially sighted
- 400 multimedia places, with 60 printers linked to them
- 371,000 books
- 2,560 periodicals, numerous press files and 11 global TV channels on 16 sets
- 5,800 maps
- 200 videodisks
- 2,100 documentary films and 100 animated films
- 10,000 audio CDs and 2,700 documentary and spoken tapes
- 1,800 musical scores
- 1,200 language-learning works for 135 languages and dialects
- 200 education and information software programs and 200 reference and multimedia CD ROMS
- 750 selected Internet sites

Further reading

Published by the Pompidou Centre:

- *Comment est née la BPI, Invention de la médiathèque*, by Jean-Pierre Seguin, 1987, 136 pages. € 10.67

- *La BPI à l'usage, 1978-1995*: comparative analysis of BPI publications, by Christophe Evans, 1998, 184 pages, € 14.48

- *Les Habitués*, by Agnès Camus, Jean Michel Cretin, Christophe Evans, Salon du livre, 2000, 328 pages. € 20.58

- *L'Utopie Beaubourg, vingt ans après*, by Jean Lauxerois, 1996, 204 pages, € 18.29

- *Collection Bonjour/Salut*. Collection of language-learning materials for rare (albeit widely spoken) languages. Materials include textbook and audio cassettes with written and spoken exercises and dialogues. Prices vary.

- *Les Livres de leur vie*, 10 booklets, 48 pages each. € 9.15
... in which writers talk about their favourite books.

documentation (6o places) and
the collection of documentary and
animation films (4o places).

The BPI is devoted to its public,
and regularly organises debates,
meetings and literary walks, and
every year holds a documentary
film festival, *Le Cinéma du réel*, that
has established an international
reputation. It likewise participates
in the Centre's interdisciplinary
activities.

Now modernised and constantly
evolving, the BPI is among the most
diversified and accessible sources
of information and culture that can
be found.

Free Internet access at the Library

The BPI is the first library in France to offer
free Internet access to its readers. Today
it has 50 Internet user places with access
to the whole web apart from e-mail services and certain sites of a racist, porno-
graphic or otherwise undesirable nature.
To book a seat, buy a ticket at the reception desk on Level 1 of the Library.
Consultation is limited to 45 minutes.
In addition, direct connection is available
at the multimedia places to about 750
sites selected for their interest per subject area.

⚠

*The success of this service often means
a lengthy wait.*

🖳 www.bpi.fr

The Library's Internet site comprises:
• the Library's catalogue
• information about the Library and its
activities
• the programme of events
• an on-line information service (bpi-
info@bpi.fr) and answers to FAQ
• a guide to about 750 selected documentary sites classified by subject area
• guides and tools
• *Oriente-express*: redirection to other
libraries in Paris and the Paris region, organised by the name of the institution,
subject area, type of collection or address.
• *Langues-info*: directory of language centres in Paris and the Paris region covering
the study of 135 languages and dialects.
• *Intervidéo*: a catalogue of 1,500 documentary films on video available to
borrowers via the French public library
network.

ℹ

• Address
Centre Pompidou
Place Georges-Pompidou, 75004 Paris

• Opening hours
Mon, Wed-Fri: 12 noon – 10 pm
Weekends and public holidays:
11 am – 10 pm
Closed Tuesdays and 1 May.

• Telephone enquiries on
+33-(0)1- 44 78 12 75, 10 am – 10 pm
weekdays (except Tuesdays) and 11 am –
10 pm weekends.

• Website: www.bpi.fr

• Fast reference service: BPI-Info can be
reached by mail (BPI-Info 75197 Paris
Cedex 04), e-mail (bpi-info@bpi.fr) or
fax (+33-(0)1-44 78 45 10).

• The blind and partially sighted should
contact BPI reception or phone 01- 44 78
12 75; volunteers (by appointment) and
adapted materials are available for reading or assistance in research.

• Groups: visitor groups can be received
in the morning by appointment (01- 44
78 43 45).

• Kiosk: a snack bar is available in the
Library.

The 400 computer terminals

Reading desks

Level 3 reading area

National Museum of Modern Art – Industrial Design Centre
One of the Finest Collections in the World

✦ L. h. escalator in the Forum. You need to buy a ticket first. Then take the escalator or lifts up to Level 4. The areas on Level 5 are reached from inside.

The MNAM-CCI has one of the finest collections of modern and contemporary art in the world. And the size of its exhibition area enables it to show it to its best advantage. Between 1,500 and 2,000 of the 50,000 items listed in its inventory are permanently on show to the public.

A visit takes in two entire storeys of the Centre, with contemporary art (1960 to the present day) on the fourth floor and modern art (1905-1960) on the fifth floor. Two displays that present not only painting,

The Grande Galerie at the MNAM, Level 4: the collections of contemporary art

was established in 1947 and an enlightened aesthete responsible for securing some of the greatest masterpieces now in the collection.

An evolving museum is above all one that keeps a constantly critical eye on the best way of presenting its works. The rooms of the Palais de Tokyo, where the MNAM was initially housed, soon became far too cramped. But the Museum had to wait nearly three decades for the construction of the new Centre of Art and Culture before it could move in during 1977. The evolution did not stop there, however. The original layout was sculpture, installations, photography, video and film but since 1992 have also integrated architecture and design.

A Museum that evolves

"A museum of living art is a museum that evolves." This dictum, still a motto for the MNAM-CCI, was formulated by Jean Cassou, director of the Museum when it

Brancusi Studio

In 1957, Constantin Brancusi donated his studio to the French state on condition that it promised to make a faithful reconstruction of it available to the public. The artist had organised his working environment like an exhibition area, with the presentation items of the works and the everyday features alike (plinths, fireplace, benches, etc.) being his creations. After several interim versions, the studio now occupies a special building designed by Renzo Piano in 1996, located in front of the Centre on Place Georges-Pompidou. Its dimensions and overhead natural light finally do justice to the place as a commemoration of the artist's genius.

ℹ️

Opening times: daily except Tuesdays and 1 May, 1 – 7 pm
Tickets for the Museum include entry to the Brancusi Studio.

revised in 1986 by Gae Aulenti, architect of the Musée d'Orsay, who sought to give more prominence to drawings and small-scale works. Then, during the renovation works in 1997-2000, Jean-François Bodin, architect of several other museums in France, embarked on a complete revamp. By transferring the administration to the exterior of the building and eliminating double-height spaces, the exhibition area was increased to 14,000 m² (150,000 sq. ft), allowing a wider insight into the Museum's collections, particularly the part devoted to architecture and design.

Change also means offering something new every visit. This is one of the great original features and driving forces of the place – changing the items on display from time to time to heighten public awareness of the range and quality of the collections while still respecting the chronological presentation of the art of the 20th and fledgling 21st centuries. This method of operation also facilitates management of the collections, and allows the Museum to respond to frequent requests for loans and to organise temporary exhibitions at the Pompidou Centre or externally, and to place certain items on deposit with other French museums.

A difficult beginning

Nevertheless, the early days were difficult for the MNAM. Before it was set up, the State had taken no interest in acquiring contemporary works. Admittedly, the Musée du Luxembourg had focused contemporary artists for more than a century, just as the Jeu de Paume was the museum for foreign schools. Neither, however, was specifically concerned with the avantgarde. Academicism prevailed in France at the time; genius was the exception. The collections for which the MNAM-CCI is famous

How the collection grows

- The MNAM-CCI has long been the very privileged beneficiary of gifts and bequests by private persons and foundations, like the recent donations by Louise and Michel Leiris, Daniel Cordier, the Matisse family, and the Scaler Foundation. Apart from their large number and wealth of major pieces of modern art, these gifts often make up real cohesive ensembles, making it almost possible to reconstruct the artists' studios.

- The Société des amis du Musée (Friends of the Museum) also plays an important part in the acquisition of works, and indeed their production. For example, when the Centre reopened, the Amis du Musée offered the MNAM-CCI a work by Mike Kelley and Tony Oursler, *The Poetics Project*.

- In 1968, a system was established whereby works of art could be given in lieu of inheritance tax. An underrated method of acquisition, it likewise contributes much to augmenting the collections.

- The Museum's purchasing committee has a specific budget for proposed new acquisitions, which are put up and voted on each year.

- Apart from purchases, the MNAM-CCI commissions works from artists, an example being *Container Zero* by Jean-Pierre Raynaud.

Further reading

Publications by the Pompidou Centre:
- *La Collection du Musée national d'art moderne II*, 1986-1996, 1997, 380 pages. € 60.98
- *La Collection d'architecture du Centre Pompidou*, 1998, 376 pages. € 60.22
- *La Collection cinématographique du Musée national d'art moderne*, 1997, 496 pages. € 68.60
- *La Collection de photographies du Musée national d'art moderne, 1905-1948*, 1997, 516 pages. € 68.60
- *La Collection design du MNAM-CCI*, 2001, 206 pages. € 39.64
- *La Collection vidéo du Musée national d'art moderne*, published by Centre Pompidou/Carré, Paris, 1992, 296 pages. € 44.21
- *La Collection du Centre Pompidou*, CD-ROM, published by Centre Pompidou/Infogrames, Paris, 1997, € 45.58

The Documentation at the MNAM-CCI

This documents 20th-century artistic creation in the visual arts, design, architecture, experimental cinema, photography and video. The Documentation comprises:

- a library with 170,000 printed works, including 70,000 exhibition catalogues and 12,000 valuable books, 6,000 periodical titles, 12,000 sales catalogues and 35,000 showroom catalogues;

- a collection of 70,000 documentary dossiers on artists, architects and designers;

- individual collections of artists, gallery owners, critics and art historians totalling 200,000 documents made up for the most part of correspondence and unedited manuscript texts;

- a photo archive preserving a great variety of media – black+white prints, slides, ektachromes, photos, glass plates, etc.

Open mainly to Museum staff for preparing exhibitions and setting up collections, the Documentation department also has a national heritage function. Its collection is at the disposal of curators, gallery owners, artists, journalists, teachers, researchers, etc.

i

Opening hours
9 30 am – 1 pm and 2 – 6 pm, Mon-Fri for professionals;
2 – 6 pm, Mon, Thurs, Fri for students.

⚠

For details of access to the Documentation, please ring +33 (0)1-44 78 47 38 for information.

Presentation of the design collection

today were virtually non-existent. And until 1969, the Museum had a very poor purchase budget.

To expand it required great determination by successive directors, but also an increasingly explicit manifestation of political will, as the creation of the Centre itself shows. Over and above that, the MNAM owes much to the generosity and public-spiritedness of collectors, artists and the Amis du Musée (Friends of the Museum) for the donation of essential works. They realised what was at stake in

establishing such a collection in France.

Purchases became a vital feature in the enlargement of the collections only from the 1970s onwards and even more in the 1980s.

From painting to architecture and design

Major collections such as those of Picasso, Kandinsky, Matisse, Braque and Bonnard, had been assembled even in the early years. Subsequent artist collections were the result of donations, and included Laurens, Rouault, Pevsner, Robert and Sonia Delaunay, Kupka, etc.

But when the Museum moved to the Pompidou Centre, it still had significant gaps. The Centre therefore decided to remedy this situation by buying key artists: such as the painters De Chirico, Mondrian, Miró, Pollock, Magritte; three-dimensional artists such as Beuys, Dubuffet, Duchamp; photographers Brassaï, Cartier-Bresson, Man Ray, etc.

Contrary to other major museums, the applied arts took some time to join the collections at the MNAM. The Centre de création industrielle (CCI, Industrial Design

Centre) had, from the outset, been hived off from the Musée des Art Décoratifs to become an integral part of the Pompidou Centre. Its architectural, design and graphic arts section were the subject of numerous exhibitions and publications. In 1992, it was decided that the CCI should merge with the MNAM in order to establish a collection of design and architecture, now displayed on the same chronological principle as that of the visual arts, on the two floors of the Museum.

Like its elder sibling, this new collection had been put together late. Those in charge were able to turn this handicap to good account by appointing the most important architects and designers of the century, a decision that allowed them better opportunities in the field of the applied arts.

A multi-faceted Museum

On the two levels of the Museum, the rooms are arranged around a central aisle. Whether devoted to a single artist or mixing and juxtaposing several artists, they present all the visual arts. On the contemporary art floor (Level 4), the rooms on the left – relative to the central aisle – are reserved for architectural models and drawings, but also for designer creations and some new-media works. On the right, the itinerary takes you through some of the most recent three-dimensional works.

On the modern art floor (Level 5), the passing of time allows for a more balanced view in explaining movements or conflicts of a period in various ways. All around the exhibition, the public can access the terraces where monumental sculptures by Picasso, Laurens, Miró, Ernst, etc. are on display.

Elsewhere on the fourth floor, visitors will discover three complementary areas of general presentation. In the Museum's gallery, temporary exhibitions spotlight the MNAM's acquisition policy, pay tribute to donors and present material relating to groups of works. The graphic art gallery focuses on this unique mode of expression in line with its importance in the Museum's collections.

The New Media area enables visitors to consult, watch and listen to artistic works using electronic media, from video to the Internet.

This brief survey would not be complete without a mention of the Brancusi Studio, a masterpiece established outside the Centre, to the right as you go out into Place Georges-Pompidou.

Finally, an indispensable, yet not so well-known, feature of the Museum is Documentation. This is a library, photo archive and heritage collection in one. It is open to all researchers, and for the Museum's curators constitutes a vital tool in preparing exhibitions and establishing collections.

Rich and multi-faceted, the National Museum of Modern Art and Industrial Design Centre has only a small part of its holdings on display. It is therefore essential for it to replace the display from time to time. The visitor thus never gets the impression on repeated visits that he/she is retreading a well-beaten track and admiring the same works each time.

Above and right:
*Presentation of
historic collections
on Level 5*

🖥 **www.centrepompidou.fr**

Apart from information of displays at the Museum, recent acquisitions and topical updates, the website includes:
- the catalogue of the Documentation;
- the New Media encyclopaedia (www. newmedia.arts.org), a European project with texts in French, English and German;
- Netart, which provides virtual exhibitions of works conceived for the Internet and commissions established in collaboration with international institutions.

ⓘ

For details of access, opening hours, tickets and rates, guided tours, groups and conferences, please refer to the relevant headings in *From A to Z (pp. 154 ff.)*.

André Derain

1880, Chatou (France) –
1954, Garches (France)

The Thames Embankment, 1905-1906

Oil on canvas, 81 x 100 cm
Gift of Marcelle Bourdon in 1990
AM 1990-202

Best known for his pre-World War I
work, André Derain continued to
paint postwar and to surprise other
artists to the day he died (1954).
An associate of Matisse from 1899,
then influenced by Picasso, Derain
was seen as the great regulator
between the two giants. Following
a trip to Italy, he returned to classical
sources, and his painting abandoned
the avantgarde in favour of a more
traditional style. The critics disowned
him, and he gradually retreated into
isolation after 1945.

    The Thames Embankment, which
dates from 1905, is a kind of snap-
shot of life. Inspired by Turner, its
heightened colours create "forms
outside objects considered real"
(A. Derain). The mastery of composition, arranged on a diagonal plane,
lends great force to the rapidly
sketched figures crossing the scene.

Georges Rouault ➤

1871, Paris (France) – 1958, Paris (France)

Girl at the Mirror, 1906

Water colour on card, 70 x 55.5 cm
Purchased in 1952
AM 1795 D

In Rouault, prostitutes (a subject he
tackled from 1903 to 1914) symbolise
human degradation. Moralistic and
devout, Rouault did not revel in his
vice like Lautrec but lamented the
tragedy of his fate. This version in
particular, which brings out contrasts
and exploits all the subtleties of
water colours, suggests the transparency of stained glass, removing
all the vulgarity from the subject
and leaving just her charm. The
prostitute becomes a modest figure
who makes no eye contact with the
viewer except via an intervening
mirror.

Georges Braque

1882, Argenteuil (France) –
1963, Paris (France)

Small Bay at La Ciotat,
1907

Oil on canvas, 36 x 48 cm
Donated by Mme Georges
Braque in 1965
AM 4298 P

In 1907 Georges Braque, who would become Picasso's partner in the Cubist years, was torn between Fauvism and the influence of Cézanne. Like the latter, he set off for the south to get to grips with the light, returning with canvases with tones that were strong but already burnt by the sun. But at La Ciotat, where he passed the summer in the company of Othon Friesz, he developed an individual style. These were the final canvases of his Fauve period. Among them, *Small Bay at La Ciotat* is undoubtedly the most successful and most distinctive, thanks to the "heterogeneous use of brushwork, with clearly separate strokes applied as just a few spots so that the white background of the fine, sized canvas can show through" (G. Braque).

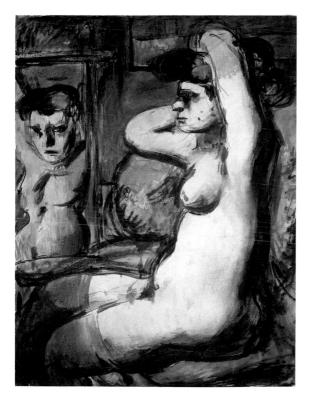

Pablo Picasso ➤

1881, Malaga (Spain) –
1973, Mougins (France)

*Woman Seated
in an Armchair*, 1910

Oil on canvas, 100 x 73 cm
Bequest of Georges Salles
in 1967
AM 4391 P

A giant of the 20th cen-
tury, Pablo Picasso is
at once an inventor and
a witness. He succeeded
in revolutionising the art
of his time while at
the same time taking
a stance in the face of
human history. The lead-
ing exponent of Cubism
along with Braque,
he explored everything
it had to offer, and in
the *Woman Seated in an
Armchair*, one of the last

Georges Braque

1882, Argenteuil (France) –
1963, Paris (France)

Woman Playing a Guitar, 1913

Oil and charcoal on canvas, 130 x 73 cm
Gift of Raoul La Roche in 1957
AM 3487 P

In *Woman Playing a Guitar*, the
deconstruction of the subject, multiple points of view and interplay
of shapes and light are typical of
Braque's Cubist painting on the
eve of the Great War. However,
following the example of the collages both he and Picasso had
begun to create, this canvas marks
the artist's desire to render material
effects and exploit the block letters of
newspapers – as if this fragmented
vision of the world needed a ballast
of realism.

Juan Gris ➤

1887, Madrid (Spain) –
1927, Boulougne-Billancourt (France)

Breakfast, 1915

Oil and charcoal on canvas, 92 x 73 cm
Purchased in 1947
AM 2678 P

From 1911, Juan Gris (born José
Victoriano Gonzàlez-Perez) devoted
himself to Cubism, and became a
kind of 'grammarian' to it. *Breakfast*
contains all the key constituent
features – the geometrisation of
objects, multiple viewpoints and
inclusion of typography. Gris adds
a theme exclusive to him, that is,
the window through which light
enters from outside and disrupts
the organisation of the still life:
the shadows cut the surface into
multiple planes, while the green

of a series of portraits
he did of Fernande – his
partner at the time – he
achieved unparalleled
compactness.

This canvas illustrates
the fragmentation of
volume into facets, even
though the image of the
person remains coherent.
The planes that make up
Fernande are so vigorous
in contrast to the virtually
flat background that she
seems to be moving –
she looks like a kind
of sculpture rendered
in paint.

of the newspaper and
surrounding objects
seems – like the brown
of the wood – to react
to the blue of the sky.
Gris' virtuosity creates
from this breakfast table
a synthetic space that
is both 'concrete and
concise' (to use his
expression).

Henri Matisse

1869, Le Cateau-Cambrésis (France) –
1954, Nice (France)

Portrait of Greta Prozor, 1916

Oil on canvas, 146 x 96 cm
Gift of the Scaler Foundation in 1982
AM 1982-426

Henri Matisse and Picasso dominated
the entire first half of the 20th century.
Matisse came into his own in 1905,
when he was already 35, after spending the summer in Collioure alongside Derain. Their 'fauves' canvases
were shown at the autumn Salon
that year, and caused a stir. In 1910
Matisse produced two large panels
called *Dance* and *Music*, models of
simplicity thanks to the use of solid
blocks of three colours. The tension
slackens in the canvases that came
out of the artist's trips to Morocco in
1912 and 1913, but with the onset of
war, black invades in his paintings.
In this period, he did a major series
of portraits that are among his most
abstract works. Greta Prozor, painted
in 1916, is one of these, sombre and
yet luminous, a tall, slender figure
like an icon against a gilt background.

Pablo Picasso

1881, Malaga (Spain) –
1973, Mougins (France)

Harlequin, 1923

Oil on canvas, 130 x 97 cm
Bequest of Baroness Eva Gourgaud in 1965
AM 4313 P

Appreciative of the world of circuses
and the atmosphere of *commedia
dell'arte*, Pablo Picasso provides us
here with a portrait of his Catalan
artist friend Jacinto Salvado as
Harlequin, wearing a costume created for Jean Cocteau. Neo-classical
in its handling, like a number of
Picasso's works after World War I,
Harlequin shows us the face of a
pensive, possibly sad man. The
partial coloration of the costume
contrasts with the attitude of gloom
that seems to imbue the subject, and
gives him life, as if his image were
returning to his mind. Here, after all
the innovations of the Cubist period,
Picasso seems to be reverting to the
traditional principles of painting.

Henri Matisse

1869, Le Cateau-Cambrésis
(France) – 1954, Nice (France)

*Decorative Figure on an
Ornamental Background,*
1925-1926

Oil on canvas, 130 x 98 cm
Purchased in 1938
AM 2149 P

This picture illustrates
Matisse's way of con-
trasting figure and
background, three-
dimensional depth
and two-dimensional
decorative space.

The body, in the
manner of the sculp-
tures Matisse was doing
in the same period,
is placed in front of a
fabric and on a carpet
whose motifs dissolve
perspective: the potted
tree, the mirror and the
basket of lemons seem absorbed into
a single plane. Only the body of
the woman, composed of contrasted
volumes and picked out with a black
outline, restores a certain sense of
presence to them.

In this picture, Matisse was exper-
imenting with new ways of handling
colour and the nude, while at the same
time reverting to a degree of simpli-
fication that recalls his 1914-1917
period. The work was an instant
critical success.

Constantin Brancusi ▼

1876, Pestisani (Rumania) – 1957, Paris (France)

Sleeping Muse, 1910

Polished bronze, 16 x 25 x 18 cm
Gift of Baroness Renée Irana Frachon in 1963
AM 1374 S

Familiar with the simplicity of
African sculpture, Rumanian sculptor Constantin Brancusi sought to
reveal a new kind of reality in sculpture. His work, which heralds all

modern sculpture generally, was quite independent of any movement, especially the Cubists, because Brancusi took a natural, cosmic world as his guide and all intellectual formalism was alien to him. Very soon after his arrival in Paris in 1904, Brancusi endeavoured to carve within the block, stone, marble or wood, from which his sculptures – like the *Sleeping Muse* – seem to be extricating themselves. The marble original of the *Muse* already reflects his efforts to eradicate any distinctive features of the model: the sculpture looks like the essence of the face, deprived of the neck as well, the ultimate link with the rest of the body. The bronze casts (five of them exist, two of which are at the MNAM-CCI) are distinguishable by tiny details. Here the patina of the hair reminds us that this sculpture is not the image of a spirit but sublimates the features of a model.

Marc Chagall

1887, Vitebsk (Russia) –
1985, Saint-Paul-de-Vence (France)

To Russia, the Donkeys and the Others,
1911
Oil on canvas, 157 x 122 cm
Gift of the artist in 1953
AM 2925 P

In Paris, which he reached during summer 1910, Marc Chagall was homesick for his native land. A year later, gradually casting off the influences of the Parisian avantgarde, he began to delve into his memory for images of his homeland. Here, in a universe that was unreal yet readily identifiable, he painted his father, peasants, an isba (wooden house), and the farm animals. In the context of the violent colour contrasts and Cubist influence on the presentation, this rural subject became a dream, a painful but idealised memory.

Vassily Kandinsky

1866, Moscow (Russia) –
1944, Neuilly-sur-Seine (France)

*Mit dem schwarzen Bogen
[With the Black Bow]*, 1912

Oil on canvas, 189 x 198 cm
Donated by Nina Kandinsky, 1976
AM 1976-852

Russian artist Vassily Kandinsky, who acquired French citizenship in 1939, was a revolutionary in the art of painting. He came to painting relatively late (nearing 30), but gradually repudiated the obligation of representation in favour of erasing all possible references to reality. Whether he is or is not recognised as the inventor of abstraction, he was one of its most brilliant exponents. Among the works in the substantial collection owned by the MNAM-CCI, *With the Black Bow* is undoubtedly an exceptional piece. It is both a synthesis of the work he had already accomplished and a foretaste of what was to come. In his lifetime,

however, the artist considered it out of date, and it remained neglected until it was shown in Paris in 1937. The black bow is incidentally the yoke of a troika that is often present in his canvases.

Vassily Kandinsky

1866, Moscow (Russia) –
1944, Neuilly-sur-Seine (France)

Gelb-Rot-Blau [Yellow-Red-Blue], 1925

Oil on canvas, 128 x 201.5 cm
Donated by Nina Kandinsky, 1976
AM 1976-856

From 1922 to 1933, Vassily Kandinsky lived in Germany, teaching at the Bauhaus. In 1925, the Bauhaus moved from Weimar to Dessau. This was also the year that Kandinsky nuanced his compositions with curves and gradations of colour.

In *Yellow-Red-Blue*, the geometrical lines on the left contrast with the free forms on the right. Kandinsky thus pursues his exploration

of an aesthetic of complexity and asserts his capacity to revive a non-figurative formal style. Drawing away from Bauhaus-trained Neo-Plasticists, Russian Constructivists, Malevich and Mondrian, he created a colourist style where shapes are born and die in a chaos of life.

František Kupka

1871, Opočno (Austro-Hungary; now Czech Republic) –
1957, Puteaux (France)

Vertical Planes I, 1912-1913
Oil on canvas, 150 x 94 cm
Purchased in 1936
JP 807 P

A Symbolist and abstract artist, Kupka paints vertical planes in this picture, detached from any explicit reference to nature and the traditional organisation of a picture. They are as if suspended in an indeterminate space, and seem to be moving steadily away from the viewer. Yet according to Kupka, the inspiration is figurative and of a Symbolist nature: "The vertical line is like a man standing." The vertical planes also evoke the keys of a piano, like the motifs of his *Nocturnes*, because Kupka was at the same time fascinated by music as an expression of pure spirituality.

Fernard Léger

1881, Argentan (France) –
1955, Gif-sur-Yvette (France)

The Wedding, c. 1911

Oil on canvas, 257 x 206 cm
Gift of Alfred Flechtheim, 1937
AM 2146 P

Fernand Léger was one of the most
singular artists of the 20th century.
At the start of his career, his style was
in the same vein as that of his Cubist
friends. Yet, the subject matter was
different, as were the vivid colours,
the depth of field, the dynamism of
the work and, above all, the tubular
forms that are quite his own.

In *The Wedding*, Léger's work
is less close to Braque and Picasso
than to Robert Delaunay, Gleizes
and Le Fauconnier, in whom the
same rounded, scarcely coloured
forms framing the scene also occur.
In the centre is a hieratic couple,
and all round them the procession,
the village and the road are rendered
in lively colours and from multiple
viewpoints to give a busy scene.

Sonia Delaunay

1885, Gradizhsk (Russia) –
1979, Paris (France)

Electrical Prisms, 1914

Oil on canvas, 250 x 250 cm
Purchased 1958
AM 3606 P

Ukrainian-born French painter
Sonia Delaunay [née Terk] was
a pioneer in the applied arts and
abstraction. Her name is always
associated with that of her husband.
A painter of colour and 'simul-
taneous contrasts,' she also applied
her motifs to gowns, scarves, waist-
coats, etc. All periods of her work
are represented in the MNAM-CCI
collection, thanks to a major donation by the artist.

Electrical Prisms, acquired by
Jean Cassou, is a masterwork
of what is known as her 'Orphic'
period: painting itself became the
sole subject of the work, and the
variations of light seem fixed to the
canvas. The whole prism is broken
down into forms and associations
that allow the infinite energy of light
to circulate.

Giorgio De Chirico

1888, Volos (Greece) – 1978, Rome (Italy)

Ritratto premonitore di Guillaume Apollinaire [Premonitory Portrait of Guillaume Apollinaire], 1914

Oil on canvas, 81.5 x 65 cm
Purchased in 1975
AM 1975-52

A classical bust sporting dark glasses, fancy baking tins, a shadow-graph silhouette of Apollinaire on a background of Veronese green, abrupt perspectives that give the impression of being at the bottom of a box and yet open to an arch on the right – that is the intriguing composition that De Chirico offers the viewer. The title itself [*Premonitory Portrait of Guillaume Apollinaire*] makes it all the more intriguing, as does the white semi-circle on the poet's head marking the precise spot where he would be wounded two years later, during the Great War. Hovering between classical painting and avantgarde vision, the painter followed his hallucinations to devise a 'metaphysical' work. It became a major reference point for Surrealism and the first half of the 20th century.

Francis Picabia ◥

1879, Paris (France) – 1953, Paris (France)

Udnie, 1913

Oil on canvas, 290 x 300 cm
Purchased in 1948
AM 2874 P

Composed on his return from New York, *Udnie* is one of Francis Picabia's finest canvases. The enigmatic title evokes a dancer he met on the liner bringing him back to Europe. Possibly influenced by the Italian Futurists, the work indicates how far Picabia had moved away from the Cubists. The work is dominated by cool colours and hard forms that open out in the middle into an outpouring of warmer colours. Bearing out that all description is out of the question for Picabia, this work illustrates an emotion and its memory in a more or less abstract fashion.

put their works on show every year. The trainer would thus be the jury or the organisers and the performing dogs the artists that submit their work to their judgment. As the mention of a fictitious date and Picabia's own admission bear out, the picture was painted, like all the others, to catch the eye, hold the attention and stir up debate.

Francis Picabia ◄

1879, Paris (France) – 1953, Paris (France)

Animal trainer, 1923
Gloss paint on canvas
250 x 200 cm
Purchased in 1998
AM 1998-174

In *Animal Trainer*, Picabia shows simple silhouettes treated as contrasting solid blocks. They are notably garish since the painter has substituted industrial gloss paint in gaudy colours for the traditional oil paints. The reduced palette is more characteristic of a poster than a painting. Like Duchamp in New York, Picabia was at odds with the Parisian Salons where painters

Kasimir Malevich ➤

1878, Kiev (Russia) –
1935, Leningrad
(Russia, USSR)

[Black] Cross, 1915

Oil on canvas, 80 x 79.5 cm
Gift of the Scaler
and Beaubourg
foundations, 1980
AM 1980-1

A Ukranian of Polish
origin, painter, writer
and philosopher Kasi-
mir Malevich carried
out basic research into
forms, declaring from
1915, in connection with
his first abstract works:
"I've gone beyond
zero, to reach creation,
that is, Suprematism." He painted
a series of minimal black geometric
units on a white background, each
of which derives from the square.

In their different versions, the
'Crosses' – this one being the oldest –
vibrate with the tension that invests
the space of the canvas, and their
irregular arms remove any rigidity
from the work. From 1935, the
works vanished into various vaults,
remaining there until a retrospective
in 1958 'rediscovered' Malevich's
work for the West. It had an immedi-
ate influence on the avantgarde
and the Minimalists.

Theo van Doesburg
[Christian Emil Marie Küpper]

1883, Utrecht (Netherlands) –
1931, Davos (Switzerland)

Composition X, 1918

Oil on canvas, 64 x 43 cm
Purchased in 2001 with the help of the
Scaler Westbury Foundation, the Scaler
Foundation and the Fonds du Patrimoine
AM 2001-44

Theo van Doesburg was an architect,
painter, poet and thinker rolled into
one. Influenced by Cézanne and im-
pressed by the writings of Kandinsky
and Apollinaire, he was, with Mondrian in particular, the creator of the
De Stijl group as well as the theoretician of abstraction and one of its
great artists. In 1918, he painted a
series called *Compositions*, and *Composition X* is one of these. As in the
other canvases, it involves progressively stylising a figurative subject.
Here, starting from a series of studies
of his mistress, he delivers a final
version stylised to the point where
each element of the original image is
converted into rectangles. Thus all
that remains is the dynamic of black,
grey and white surfaces, arranged
orthogonally on the same plane.

Marcel Duchamp

1887, Blainville-Crevon
(France) – 1968, Paris
(France)

Nine Malic Moulds,
1914-1915
Glass, lead, oil painting,
coated steel
66 x 101.2 cm
Donated in lieu of
inheritance tax, 1997
AM 1997-95

Nine Malic Moulds
forms part of *The
Bride Stripped Bare
by her Bachelors, even.*
To be precise, it is
the part representing the bachelors,
the males come to woo the bride,
who discharge a gas, a symbol of
their virility, via a system of tubes.
The Bride, which Duchamp left
unfinished in 1923, is nonetheless
highly precise in all its details.
Thus, these moulds are just 'coffins,'
"nine outside envelopes of the
casts of nine different uniforms and
liveries," the perspectives of which
the artist had studied meticulously,
each mould – except for one –
having an elliptical section. A very
sophisticated work which Duchamp
was always delighted to
show with the casualness
that suited his subject.

By this act, he was asserting that
any object at all 'chosen' by the artist
is elevated to the status of a work
of art. A manifesto of readymades,
Fountain is considered as the genesis
of current art. This was where a
number of revolutions and artistic
excesses of our time all began.

The work was shown again
in 1950, more than 30 years later.
The original piece having been lost,
Duchamp signed a replica, followed
by other editions that enabled the
work to be included in the world's
great collections.

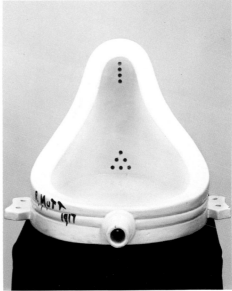

Marcel Duchamp

1887, Blainville-Crevon (France)
– 1968, Paris (France)

Fountain, 1917/1964
White enamel, paint
63 x 48 x 35 cm
Purchased in 1986
AM 1986-295

From a simple urinal
that he signed 'R Mutt,'
Marcel Duchamp made
a *Fountain* in 1917. The
object would engender
almost a century of cre-
ation and controversy.

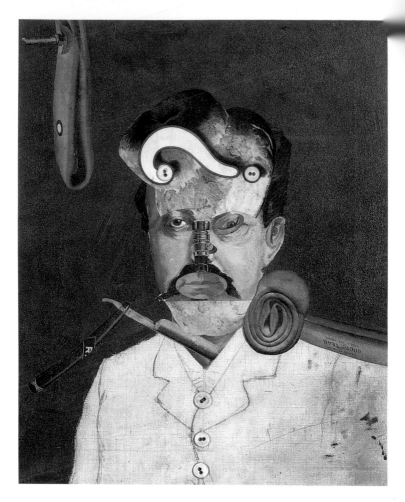

George Grosz

1893, Berlin (Germany) –
1959, Berlin (Germany)

*Remember Uncle August,
the Unhappy Inventor,* 1919

Oil, pencil, various materials
49 x 39.5 cm
Purchased in 1977
AM 1977-562

Shown at the first major international Dada exhibition in Berlin
in 1920, this work is made up of
disparate elements that seem to
be united by chance on a simple
painted or sketched-in background.
For Dada George Grosz, it was a
way to criticise traditional painting,
the very conditions of art and,
beyond that, the cultural ideology
developed by bourgeois society.
Written on the frame, the monitory
'Remember Uncle August, the
Unhappy Inventor' is a reminder
that this society was unable to pre-
vent the Great War.

Raoul Hausmann

1886, Vienna (Austria) –
1971, Limoges (France)

*Der Geist unserer Zeit
(Mechanischer Kopf) [The Spirit
of Our Time (Mechanical Head)]*, 1919
A wooden hairdresser's dummy
and various materials
32.5 x 21 x 20 cm
Purchased in 1974
AM 1974-6

This wooden hairdresser's dummy
with various objects attached to it –

a purse, a number 22 disc, a metal
noggin, a small jewellery box,
a film reel container, the stem of
a pipe, a wooden ruler, a camera
accessory – illustrates the imperson-
ality of human kind. "Their faces
are just images created by the
hairdresser," explains Hausmann.
Satirising the petty bourgeois out-
look, with a love-hate relationship
for a mechanised civilisation but
attacking the dehumanisation
of our society, the black humour
of Dada amuses even as it despairs.

Max Ernst ➤

1891, Brühl (Germany) –
1976, Paris (France)

Ubu Imperator, 1923

Oil on canvas
81 x 65 cm
Gift of the Fondation pour
la Recherche Médicale, 1984
AM 1984-281

A work from the early
days of Surrealism,
Ubu Imperator is the
heir to Cubist collages.
It is an assemblage
of heterogeneous ele-
ments which together
make up an alternative
reality. This massive
shape, a Leaning
Tower of Pisa, spin-
ning top and man all
in one, symbolises
a grotesque power
in the style of Jarry's
Ubu, whose heavy inertia is at vari-
ance only with the whirling of his
shadow. In fact, this strange figure
evokes the prestige of paternal
authority, the sexual act and visual
creation – but it is a prestige that
falters. A year previous to the publication of the *Surrealist Manifesto*,
Max Ernst was here mapping out
the route he was taking, blending
symbols of childhood and thoughts
on the act of painting.

Max Ernst

1891, Brühl (Germany) – 1976, Paris (France)

*Physical Culture, or,
Death as You Like It*, 1929

Engravings cut up and pasted, 11.2 x 8.2 cm
Gift of Carlo Perrone, 1999
AM 1999-3(15)

During his stay in the Ardèche in 1928,
Max Ernst did 150 collages based on
printed reproductions. He integrated
them all, including *Physical Culture,
or, Death as You Like It*, in his novel
La Femme 100 têtes, which appeared
at the end of 1929. The ensemble was
never shown as an integrated whole
and is now dispersed. The forty
plates given to the MNAM-CCI give
some idea of the collage novel that
Ernst invented. They are images
with no text (the captions being later
additions suggested by Breton) or
narrative logic. The unity derives
from the force of the visual and poetic
hallucination, which constitutes the
very substance of the dream.

Joan Miró

1893, Barcelona (Spain) – 1983, Palma de Mallorca (Spain)

Siesta, 1925

Oil on canvas
113 x 146 cm
Purchased in 1977
AM 1977-20

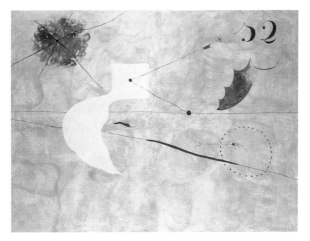

Later associated with the Surrealists, Joan Miró himself also tried to 'achieve poetry' in painting. Resident in Paris from 1920 (though spending the summers in Catalonia), he went through a period of 'magic realism' before developing his 'dream painting' series (1925-1928).

Siesta is one of the latter. It is a complex work. Over and beyond the unified background (typical of this period), it draws inspiration from the landscape of the family farm at Montroig. But, in synthesising the different figurative elements (a woman, the sun, a bather, the crests of a mountain, a sundial, etc.), Miró allows a vibrant blue to permeate the canvas and turn the scene into a dream-like vision.

Joan Miró

1893, Barcelona (Spain) – 1983, Palma de Mallorca (Spain)

[Collage], 1929

Tarred sheet, various cutout and pasted papers, wire, bits of rag, ink and pencil
74.4 x 73.7 x 7 cm
Purchased in 1996
AM 1996-394

As his work steadily evolved following his arrival in Paris in 1920, Miró gave up his huge homogeneous backgrounds strewn with a number of signs – though this would constitute the basis of his future work – to return to reality (1928-1929). He then turned to collages and assemblages of unprocessed elements in a kind of anti-painting.

This collage has all the austerity of a work not improved with drawings. Miró introduces two basic elements of his handiwork – a rough (exclusively tactile) materiality, and abstract and random shapes.

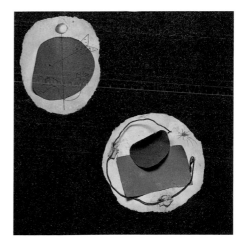

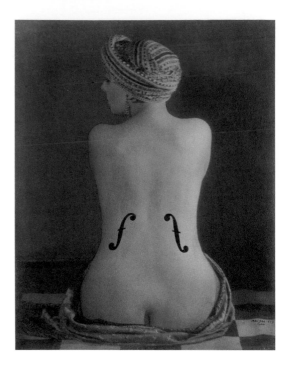

Man Ray [Emmanuel Radnitzky]
1890, Philadelphia (USA) –
1976, Paris (France)

Ingres' Violin, 1924
Gelatin silver print with graphite and
Indian ink highlights, on a paper backing
31 x 24.7 cm
Purchased in 1993
AM 1993-117

Aleksandr Rodchenko ◀
1891, St Petersburg (Russia) –
1956, Moscow (Russia, USSR)

*Cover project for the Constructivist
anthology* 'Viste miena vsiekh,' 1924
Photomontage, gelatin silver print
23.5 x 16.5 cm
Gift of Mouli Rodchenko, 1981
AM 1981-577

Man Ray's most famous work,
Ingres' Violin was based on Ingres'
picture *La Baigneuse Valpinçon* (1808),
and is a reminder that Ingres was
a keen violinist. This photo of
the model Kiki of Montparnasse,
on whose back Man Ray drew two
sound holes in Indian ink, is a visual
pun suggesting the photographer's
passion for the body of the young
woman. At the time Man Ray
did this work, a close and fruitful
association had existed between
photography and the avantgarde
for almost a decade and a half.
Art found a rich seam in photography, for example, when the Surrealists challenged the 'principle of
reality.'

Having announced the death of
'easel painting,' Soviet Constructivist
artist Aleksandr Rodchenko gradually turned to photography, which he
valued for its simplificatory strength.
However, he did not begin to take
photos himself until 1924, specialising up to then in photomontage,
as for this cover project for *Miena
Vsiekh*, an anthology of Constructivist poetry.
    This 'Rodchenko method' was
so popular that state publishing
houses adopted it widely. It mixes
cutouts from various magazines
with photographs specially taken
for the composition, like the walking
man, a portrait of the poet Ilya
Shisherin.

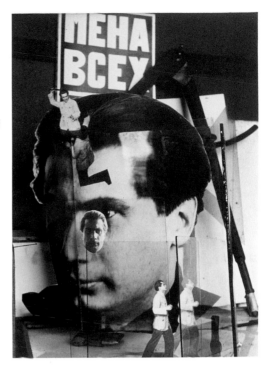

László Moholy-Nagy ◀

1895, Bácsborsód (Hungary)
– 1946, Chicago (USA)

Photogram (Self Portrait), c. 1926

Gelatin silver print
24 x 18 cm
Purchased in 1988
AM 1988-1183

The founder and theoretician of modern photography, László Moholy-Nagy is one of the most important artists of the 20th century. Linked with the Berlin avantgarde in the 1920s, he taught at the Bauhaus from 1923 to 1928, but emigrated to London (1935), then the USA (1937). He very quickly developed his style of concentrating on everyday subjects that acquire originality through high or low camera angles or other spectacular camera positions.

His most notable creations were photograms, images obtained without a camera by projecting light on to a subject placed on a sheet of light-sensitive paper – manipulations of light that he considered the 'key to photography.' This self portrait is a very fine illustration of the technique.

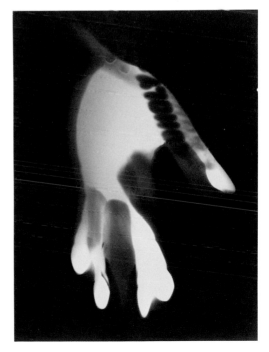

Otto Dix

1891, Untermhaus (Germany) –
1969, Singen (Germany)

Bildnis der Journalist Sylvia von Harden
[Portrait of the Journalist Sylvia von
Harden), 1926

Oil and tempera on wood, 121 x 89 cm
Purchased in 1961
AM 3899 P

Otto Dix combined a mastery of
Renaissance techniques with a taste
for caricature. He thus offers a vision
of the Weimar Republic that is precise, polished and scathing. German
society was in a state of flux at the
time. Dix spotlighted its contradictions, with its feverish excitement
and unnatural joie de vivre.

Liberated intellectual and journalist Sylvia von Harden looks out
of proportion, like a dislocated mari-
onette, her head placed on an over-
large body, her hands awkward
but appearing to embrace the world.
She bears all the stigmata of her time.

Christian Schad

1894, Miesbach (Germany) –
1982, Stuttgart (Germany)

*Portrait of Count Saint-Genois
d'Anneaucourt*, 1927

Oil on wood, 103 x 80.5 cm
Purchased in 2000
AM 2000-4

An idiosyncratic image in the Neue
Sachlichkeit (New Objectivity) vein,
the *Portrait of Count Saint-Genois
d'Anneaucourt* presents a vision of
a faltering world, the interwar years,
in which German aristocracy had
lost its bearings and was foundering
on its innate contradictions. Following the example of Otto Dix,
Christian Schad paints the spirit
of his times, though perhaps less
violently or at least with greater
objectivity. The spirit of the times
did not stop this aristocrat, a notori-
ous reveller, and his nocturnal
acolytes from savouring the social,
political and sexual degeneration of
the day. Sexuality was a favourite
theme for Schad at the time. Shown
between warm and cold colours
on different planes, the count seems
indifferent to those who surround
him here.

Pierre Chareau

1883, Bordeaux (France) –
1950, East Hampton (USA)

The Nun, 1923

Wrought, beaten iron and alabaster
171 x 45 x 55 cm
Purchased with the assistance
of the Scaler Foundation, 1995
AM 1995-1-46

French architect and designer Pierre
Chareau, creator of the famous Maison
de Verre (Glass House) in Paris, was
greatly influenced by the Cubists.
The Nun, a lamp designed in 1923,
bears evidence of this influence. It
came in three versions (a standard
lamp, table lamp and reading light).
It consists of a wooden or wrought
iron shaft beaten and shaped by
wrought-iron craftsman Louis Dalbet.
At the top is a shade made of triangular panes of alabaster reminiscent of
nuns' cornets. It was first shown in
1925, at the International Exhibition
of Decorative Arts in Paris.

Charlotte Perriand ◀

1903, Paris (France) –
1999, Paris (France)

Extending table, 1927

Aluminium, chromium-plated steel,
rubber; 72 x 180 x 91 cm
Purchased in 1994
AM 1994-1-302

Charlotte Perriand met Le Corbusier
and Pierre Jeanneret at the autumn
Salon in 1927, where she was
showing her extending table. It was
the start of a long collaboration.
Intended for her studio in the
Place Saint-Sulpice, the table is
made up of a top covered in black
rubber and an extending aluminium
frame. This rests on one side on
a case set against the wall which
houses the ball-bearings enabling
the table to be extended, on the
other side on two supports, the
front one moving as the table is
pulled out. There are two models

of this table, which has never been published.

From 1930, Charlotte Perriand was a member of the founding group of the Union des artistes modernes (Union of Modern Artists).

desire for independence is another aspect of Eileen Gray's personality that this piece reflects. It only needed the doors to be opened wide for the rest of the room to be shut off so as to afford privacy at any time.

Eileen Gray ➤

1878, Enniscorthy (Ireland) –
1976, Paris (France)

Bathroom cupboard, 1927-1929
Wooden frame with aluminium
foil, mirror, glass, cork
164 x 56 x 18 cm
Purchased in 1992
AM 1992-1-6

Irish designer Eileen Gray designed both the house she had built for herself on the Côte d'Azur and the furnishings for it. This bathroom cupboard manages to meet the double need to be both practical and comfortable. Two asymmetrical doors open on an interior mirror, shelves and drawers. Some are in glass and wood, the others – moveable and pivoting – are lined with cork to provide contrasting materials and methods of arrangement. Her

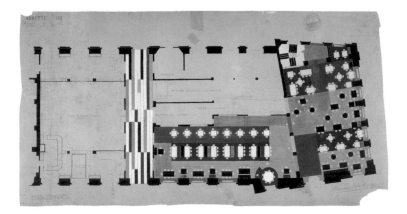

Theo van Doesburg

1883, Utrecht (Netherlands) –
1931, Davos (Switzerland)

Aubette Project:
ground-floor plan, 1927

Indian ink, gouache, black lead on print
of architect's drawing, 52.9 x 98.7 cm
Gift of the Dutch State, 1986
AM 1987-1067

The Aubette was an old guardroom
in Strasbourg that was due to be
converted into a restaurant/cinema/
dancing complex in 1922. In 1926,
the owners turned to Hans and
Sophie Arp, who in turn called
in Theo van Doesburg as a trained
architect to help them convert and
decorate the place. This ambitious
avantgarde project fizzled out ten
years later, and is now best known
through Doesburg's preparatory
drawings. They show how far the
artist was trying at the time to confer
an organic, pure and homogeneous
look on features both three-dimensional and functional.

Iakov Gheorghievich Chernikhov ◀

1889, Pavlograd (Russia) –
1951, Moscow (Russia, USSR)

Composition no. 3, 1933

Ink and gouache on card, 24 x 30 cm
Gift of Andrei Chernikhov and the Iakov
Chernikhov International Foundation, 1996
AM 1997-2-11

After graduating as an architect
and painter in 1925, Chernikhov
established in Leningrad a laboratory
of architectural forms and experimental graphic, scientific and technical art methods. A designer of
industrial buildings and teacher,
he was gradually forced into line
by socialist realism. The numerous
compendia of architectural works
he left behind show the extent to
which he was able to synthesise
Suprematism, Constructivism and
Futurism, as this design from the
Architectural Fantasies confirms.
The *Fantasies* are a collection of
101 visionary projects for towns,
skyscrapers or, as here, factories.
The drawing removes all heaviness
from the buildings, lending them
a life they would never know.

Paul Klee

1879, Münchenbuchsee
(Switzerland) –
1940, Locarno
(Switzerland)

Rhythmical, 1930
Oil on canvas
69.6 x 50.5 cm
Purchased in 1984
AM 1984-356

Paul Klee carried
on his exploration of
form at the Bauhaus,
where he taught from
1921. In this period,
he was creating
a complex system
comprising graphic
signs with symbolic
connotations. *Rhyth-
mical* is an example
of these.

Enclosed in a
moving chessboard,
a succession of
deformed squares
varying from
black to white lend rhythm to the
pictorial composition. It is an identical rhythm that does not change
until line 4, like syncopation in
the notes of a jazz theme. Klee thus
conveys existing dynamic tensions,
rendered by the use of three
non-colours, different values and
weightings vibrating against the
ochre background.

Robert Delaunay

1885, Paris (France) –
1941, Montpellier (France)

Joie de Vivre, 1930

Oil on canvas, 200 x 228 cm
Donated by Sonia and Charles Delaunay,
1964
AM 4083 P

Unlike other abstracts such as
those of the Bauhaus or De Stijl
with whom he exhibited at this
time, Robert Delaunay expresses his
Joie de vivre here by a free lyricism
that permeates the canvas. In 1930,
after a figurative period, Delaunay
returned to abstraction and here
produced one of the major pictures
of this period.

Like in his pre-war works, he
juxtaposes circles made up of the
four last colours of the rainbow
(green, yellow, orange, red). None
of them intermingle, even if sometimes spots of the same colour are
contiguous in two different shades,
a feature already apparent in some
of his wife Sonia's canvases. It is
a composition where the imbalance

is only apparent: two discs with
a black core offset the pronounced
leftward slant.

Salvador Dalí ▲

1904, Figueras (Spain) –
1989, Cadaqués (Spain)

(Partial) Hallucination.
Six Apparitions of Lenin on a Piano,
1931

Oil on canvas, 114 x 146 cm
Purchased in 1938
AM 2909 P

The most flamboyant artist of the
Surrealist group, though excluded
by them in 1938, Salvador Dalí
developed a strong link between
painting and mental images, bringing to light the urges and taboos of
the unconscious.

In *(Partial) Hallucination. Six
Apparitions of Lenin on a Piano*, he
reconstructs a vision seen in half-
sleep where portraits of Lenin
appeared to him in halos of yellow
flame. Symbolic motifs unique to
the artist fill out the picture, notably

the napkin cloak on the seated man's back and the red translucent cherries that recur on his armband. Finally, on the piano (already found in other works), sheet music is being eaten by ants. In the background, a door is ajar, opening on to a distant mountain that looks like an Easter Island figure and gives off a strange, supernatural light.

Luis Buñuel ➤

1900, Calanda (Spain) –
1983, Mexico City (Mexico)

L'Âge d'or [The Golden Age], 1930

35mm b/w film, soundtrack
Duration: 63 mins.
Donated in lieu of inheritance tax in 1989
AM 1989-F 1128

After the success of their first film, *Un chien andalou* (1929), Buñuel and Dalí obtained funds from Viscount Charles de Noailles to shoot a longer sound film in conditions closer to those of the commercial film industry.

    L'Âge d'or picks up the subject of sexual drive and its constant frustration alreadydeveloped in *Un chien andalou*. It formed part of the general theme of mad passion that was so important to the Surrealists in the 1930s. *L'Âge d'or* marks a turning point inSurrealist cinema, abandoning respectable fantasy in favour of strategies of compression achieved by editing film.

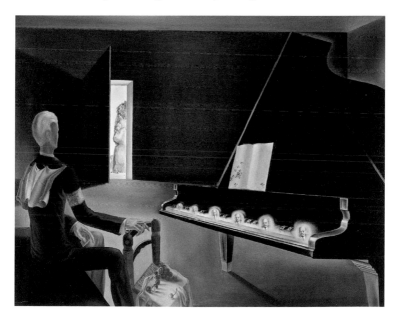

Brassaï (Gyula Halász)

1899, Brassó (Hungary) – 1984, Paris (France)

The Tower of Saint-Jacques, c. 1932-1933

Gelatin silver print, 29 x 22 cm
Purchased with the assistance of the Commission Nationale de la Photographie, 1994
AM 1994-36

Born in Transylvania in 1899, Brassaï dreamed of going to live in Paris, where he had already spent some time as a child. He finally arrived there in 1924 and began to take photos during nocturnal prowls. For him, the "photographer was a collector ... of images at the same time as of moments of emotion in his life."

Over nearly 40 years, Brassaï remained a constant observer of the city, presenting us with a wide range of visions of it, though they were always anchored in the real world, "because nothing is more surreal," he said.

The Tower of Saint-Jacques, which inspired Breton and the Surrealists, looms into the night, the lantern sticking out of scaffolding like a terrestrial beacon watching over Paris.

Pierre Bonnard

1867, Fontenay-aux-Roses (France) –
1947, Le Cannet (France)

Rear View of Nude at her Toilet, 1934

Oil on canvas, 107.3 x 74 cm
Donated in lieu of inheritance tax in 1989
AM 1989-561

Pierre Bonnard's chief interest was
in the representation of the body.
His wife, Marthe, became his sole
model, and he observed everything
she did, from the most trivial
gestures to the most intimate acts.

This rear view of her at her toilet,
which was added to the collections
in 1989, bears all the typical features
of the artist's work. As reflected
in a mirror, the nude body and its
movements have a different reality.
The range of colours, particularly
the saffron powder-like yellow,
also dematerialises how things look.
The nude thus melts into her sur-
roundings and is only noticeable
in the golden light from outside
and which is reflected off Marthe's
back.

Pablo Picasso ▲
1881, Malaga (Spain) –
1973, Mougins (France)

Secrets, 1934
Paint on size and pieces of paper stuck
on canvas, 194 x 170 cm
Donated by Marie Cuttoli, 1963
AM 4210 P

Dating from 1934, *Secrets* is the car-
toon for a tapestry that would be
woven the same year at Aubusson.
The technique is composite in that he
uses both collage, oil and gouache.
Two women of very different types
are kneeling face to face. On the left,
the silhouette of a massive body
occupies almost the entire canvas,
laden down with materials which
cover and imprison it. Its impercept-
ible eye, the features of its face and
the attitude of folded arms add to the
impression of confinement. On the
right, dismissed to the edge of the
frame, is a young woman, completely
white, surrounded by a simple black
outline, beautiful and naked. She appears to be deferring to the woman
facing her, listening to secrets, perhaps.

Pablo Picasso

1881, Malaga (Spain) –
1973, Mougins (France)

Dawn Serenade, 1942
Oil on canvas, 195 x 265 cm
Gift of the artist, 1947
AM 2730 P

This picture is considered Picasso's masterpiece during the years of the Occupation. It is a caricature version of the traditional themes of serenades and odalesques. Although the two people in it are female, Picasso depicts here not a salacious situation so much as confinement and oppression. The stripes of the floor and the cover, and the vanishing points of the perspective likewise intensify the claustrophobic, incarcerated look of the scene. Less offered up than stripped bare, the prone woman seems dead on a torture bed. Opposite her, her keeper, whose forms are as sharp as knives, holds her mandolin as you hold a truncheon. Finally, the contrast of dark and strident colours reinforces even more the general impression of unease.

Balthus
[Balthazar Klossowski de Rola]

1908, Paris (France) –
2001, Rossinière (Switzerland)

Alice, 1933

Oil on canvas, 162.3 x 112 cm
Purchased with the assistance of the
Fonds du Patrimoine, 1995
AM 1995-205

While still very young, Balthus developed a deliberately figurative style close to the Renaissance in colouring and stylistic features. The dream-like quality of his work, drawing on his childhood and adolescence, brought him close to the Surrealists, but his appeal to the Parisian public was quite independent of any movement. It began with his first exhibition (in 1934) and steadily grew to become a world-wide reputation.

Alice is one of his emblematic works where the contrast between an unobtrusive décor and the sensuality of the young girl only serves to reinforce the provocative presence: with glazed look, she offers her breasts, reveals her sex and caresses her hair more than she brushes it.

Julio González ◂

1876, Barcelona (Spain) –
1942, Arcueil (France)

Woman Doing her Hair I, c. 1931

Wrought iron, 168.5 x 54 x 27 cm
Gift of Roberta González, 1953
AM 951 S

Relatively unknown, Julio González was the pioneer of sculpture in iron. His techniques and sculptural vision revolutionised 20th-century art.

He came to Paris from Catalonia in 1900, and in 1918 discovered welding, which would become the focus of his oeuvre. A friend of Picasso, he collaborated with him between 1928 and 1931, gaining therefrom greater freedom of form. González's real originality became evident with this piece from 1931. Each plane of the work refers to a component feature of the figure represented, reinterpreted through shaping the iron. As the artist intended, the surfaces are handled in such a way that none of them masks any other.

Victor Brauner ▼

1903, Piatra-Neamt (Rumania) –
1966, Paris (France)

Mr K's Powers of Concentration, 1934
Oil on canvas, celluloid, paper, wire
148.5 x 295 cm
Purchased in 1991
AM 1991-47

The museum possesses a substantial collection of this underrated artist, who was for a long time a fellow traveller of the Surrealists and whose work is less interesting for claims of style than the force of the inspiration. Rumanian-born Victor Brauner spent the second part of his life in France. He painted this work there on his first visit (1930-1934). Mr K is a recurrent figure in Brauner, the apotheosis of human folly, subservient to fascist diktats. In this diptych which isn't one, Mr K and his double are a dual expression of the same archetype.

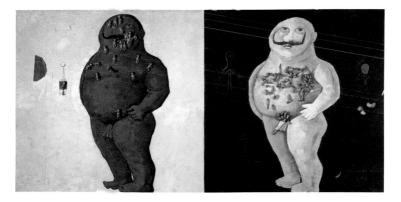

Fernand Léger

1881, Argentan (France) –
1955, Gif-sur-Yvette (France)

Composition with Two Parrots, 1935-1939
Oil on canvas, 400 x 480 cm
Gift of the artist, 1953
AM 3026 P

Workers, the world of industry, paid
holidays ... these themes are ever
present in the works of Fernand
Léger on his return from the USA
after the war, even though he had
also tackled them from the 1930s
in huge canvases where the human
figure was magnified.

Occupying virtually the whole
surface of the canvas, massive and
gentle, a blend of the arabesque
and hieratic, the people in the *Composition with Two Parrots* seem to be
responding to the pillars and clouds
surrounding them. This monumental
painting was the occasion for numerous studies, and the painter himself
considered it one of his most accomplished works.

René Magritte ▼

1898, Lessines (Belgium) –
1967, Brussels (Belgium)

Steps of Summer, 1938
Oil on canvas, 60 x 73 cm
Purchased in 1991
AM 1991-138

René Magritte produced an original
Surrealist output despite his turbu-
lent relationship with André Breton's
group. In 1938, when he was endeavouring to resolve the 'problems'
posed by the poetic evocation of
certain objects (glass, umbrellas, etc.),
he painted this painting, which is
a meditation on the relationship between art and measurement. Ancient
Greece set the canons of beauty by
relying on a mathematical principle.
Then, in the same rational vein,
the Italian Renaissance invented
perspective. The Belgian painter reinterpreted these fundamental myths
by turning them upside down. The
anatomy is reassembled on the basis
of discrete standards, and perspective is re-invented by the juxtaposition of clouds and cubes of sky.

Henri Cartier-Bresson ◀

1908, Chanteloup-en-Brie (France)

In the Calle Cuauhtemoctzin,
Mexico City, 1934

Gelatin silver print, 39.7 x 29.4 cm
Purchased in 1990
AM 1990-140

Henri Cartier-Bresson studied painting in the studios of André Lhote in 1927 and 1928, but it was a Leica he bought in 1931 that became his lifelong passion. He travelled the world, endeavouring to catch the 'decisive moment' in photos that he never cropped on printing, photos where composition and geometry took first place. He was involved in founding the Magnum photo agency in 1947, after also making a number of short films. By this time, he already had an almost mythical reputation as, thinking he'd disappeared, MoMA had devoted a posthumous retrospective to him in 1946. Since then, major exhibitions have succeeded one another across the world.

The present work, one of his first negatives, represents a Mexican prostitute leaning through the flap of a shutter like a chameleon. A master of composition, Cartier-Bresson said in connection with this photo that it is necessary to "place your camera in space in relation to the object."

Minotaure

Vol. 6, issue no. 12-13, May 1939,
Cover: André Masson
Albert Skira publishers, Paris
Art and literary review
Director: Albert Skira
Editorial committee:
André Breton, Maurice Heine,
Pierre Mabille
32 x 32 cm
Documentation section,
MNAM-CCI

Founded by Albert Skira, the periodical *Minotaure* was published from June 1933 to May 1939 – 13 issues in eleven instalments. The covers were designed (in chronological order) by Picasso, Gaston-Louis Roux, Derain, Borès, Duchamp, Miró, Dalí, Matisse, Magritte, Ernst and Masson. Poetry, three-dimensional arts, music, architecture, ethnography and mythology, entertainment, essays and psycho-analytical observations featured.

With input from André Breton (and Paul Eluard from issues 3-4 on), the review became and remained a beacon of the Surrealist movement.

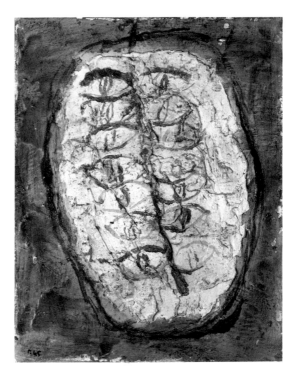

Hans Bellmer

1902, Katowice (Poland; formerly in
German Silesia) – 1975, Paris (France)

The Doll, 1949

Coloured gelatin silver print, 101 x 101 cm
Gift of Daniel Cordier, 1989
AM 1989-221

Born in Silesia in 1902, Hans Bellmer
broke with German society very
early. He abandoned his engineering
studies to live the life of a bohemian
in Berlin. In 1933, he abandoned his
family and the advertising company
he had founded. And, in order "not
to do anything that could be useful
to the state," he decided to construct
a doll 'limb by limb' (H. Bellmer).
Violent, unreal assemblages followed,
which he initially photographed
to document his work as a sculptor,
the negatives gradually acquiring the
status of independent works.

Here, the doll brings together
two pairs of legs around a belly in
the form of a ball. It is photographed
placed against a tree behind, with
a man lurking close by.

Jean Fautrier

1898, Paris (France) –
1964, Châtenay-Malabry (France)

Head of a Hostage, 1945

Oil on paper mounted on canvas, 35 x 27 cm
Purchased in 2001
AM 2001-35

This *Head of a Hostage* belongs to
50 works that Jean Fautrier showed
in Paris in his *Hostages* exhibition,
which was a major event. It is a war
work and homage to its martyrs, as
well as being a cry of denunciation
of summary executions. The technique used (a mixture of whiting, oil,
water colour, ink, size and pigments)
brings out acutely the terror that the
head expresses. It also engenders
alarm in the viewer that the fragility
of line seems no match for the violence of the work. A timeless statement, Fautrier's *Heads of Hostages*
loom up from the depth of a night
of horror.

Roberto Matta [Echaurren]

1911, Santiago (Chile)

Misdemeanours, c. 1941-1942

Pencil and wax crayons on paper
57.2 x 72.7 cm
Purchased in 1985
AM 1985-44

Eluding all classification, Chilean-born French painter Roberto Matta constituted in many respects a link between French Surrealism and American abstraction. Duchamp was already claiming in 1938 that he had discovered "regions of space hitherto unexplored by art." *Misdemeanours* belongs to a series from 1940 to 1944, whose theme of conflict foreshadows the work to come. These figurations – both painted and drawn – of bodies and spaces in mutation, tell of visionary combats involving clashes between pleasure and sexual violence, life and death. Mixed at the dry tip of a graphite pencil, the red wax crayon renders admirably the violent flows these fictions are subjected to.

Antonin Artaud ▼

1896, Marseille (France) –
1948, Ivry-sur-Seine (France)

Portrait of Jany de Ruy, 1947

Pencil and coloured chalks in paper, 65 x 50 cm
Purchased in 1987
AM 1987-554

The drawings of Antonin Artaud – an artistic 'rebel,' who for a long time was shut up in a mental hospital – are for the most part

Jean Dubuffet

1901, Le Havre (France) – 1985, Paris (France)

Dhôtel Tinted in Apricot, 1947

Oil on canvas, 116 x 89 cm
Purchased with the assistance
of the Scaler Foundation, 1981
AM 1981-501

preserved at the MNAM-CCI,
which has regularly put successive
acquisitions on show. These drawings, similar in certain aspects
to those of Michaux, Dubuffet
or Giacometti, have an impact that
goes beyond the necessity to create.
They are the rebellion of a body and
mind dispossessed of themselves,
in a bid to reintegrate a devastated
identity.

In the *Portrait of Jany de Ruy*,
script and drawing go hand in hand.
A continuous flow of inscriptions
invades the space as if to ward off
ill fortune. A face entirely covered
with nodules and symbolic motifs
is accentuated by a line in blue chalk,
as if this young woman's head had
just swallowed the writing or were
just extricating itself from it.

This picture is one of the last of a
series of portraits of artist and writer
friends that Dubuffet did in 1946 and
1947. He uses a new idiom close to
the graffiti that the artist had worked
on from 1942. Rejecting any kind of
cultural system, Dubuffet developed
a liking for 'primitivism,' and sought
to paint portraits where psychology
and individuality are excluded.
Dhôtel Tinted in Apricot is a portrait
that is both frightening and sensual.
At first glance, the style seems child-
ish, but this emaciated face is that
of a corpse. The subject of the painting evokes a scarification in which
the knife penetrates furthest where
it would penetrate a layer of skin.

Robert Doisneau

1912, Gentilly (France) – 1994, Paris (France)

Dance for Josette's Twenty Years, 1945

Gelatin silver print, 29.7 x 39.1 cm
Purchased in 1989
AM 1989-40

Robert Doisneau is a believer in humanist photography, observant of the lives of ordinary people in situations that the artist sometimes sets up.

He first published his pictures in 1932. At an exhibition of French photography at MoMA in 1948, he was the best represented exhibitor. Even though he produced the key part of the work that made him famous between 1945 and 1960, he roved the streets with a sharp, observing eye for people for more than 60 years, particularly in the Paris suburb he came from. Over and above the impression of holiday and delight emanating from this photo, Doisneau also records a social milieu. It is a dance, certainly, but one taking place on an embankment between the railway and a line of tenement buildings.

Gisèle Freund

1912, Berlin (Germany) –
2000, Paris (France)

Pierre Bonnard, Le Cannet, 1946

Colour print on Kodak paper
36 x 27 cm
Gift of the artist, 1992
AM 1992-196

A middle-class Berliner by birth, Gisèle Freund took a very early interest in photography. In 1933, she took off for Paris and discovered colour. From 1938 to 1940, she did numerous portraits. Fleeing from France in 1940, she

embarked on a long series of repor-
tages in South America for European
and American magazines. After the
war, she returned to Paris to live.

This was when she took this portrait of Pierre Bonnard, at Le Cannet
(Cannes). It shows an elderly man
with a lost look, without any attempt
at dressing up or staging – a reminder of how much the role of
a photograph was for Freund to
"be a sensitive instrument through
which a personality can be revealed."

Henri Laurens ▲
1885, Paris (France) – 1954, Paris (France)

Morning, 1944
Bronze, 118 x 123 x 118 cm
Donated by Claude Laurens, 1967
AM 1618 S

A friend of Braque's, Henri Laurens
made the acquaintance of Picasso
and Léger in 1911. Attracted
to Cubism for a time, he strove
to adapt Cubist rules to volume.
Then forms became more identifiable, Maillol-style curves reappeared,
and the topic of woman was ever
present. From 1939, the evolution
resumed; volumes henceforth
bulged more, and the human
figure was interpreted more freely.
With the onset of war, Laurens'
work became more sombre
and appeared to lose its vigour.
Morning, dating from 1944, could
indicate a degree of revival. The
sculpture seems nonetheless still
burdened with the weight that
prevents this woman from picking
herself up entirely.

Wols [Wolfgang Schulze]

1913, Berlin (Germany) – 1951, Paris (France)

Butterfly Wing, 1947

Oil on canvas, 55 x 46 cm
Gift of René de Montaigu, 1979
AM 1979-255

Wols' work glides "towards an inter-mediate world where the imaginary and the real cease to be contradictory" (W. Haftmann). This applies also to the *Butterfly Wing*, a symbol of fragility and the ephemeral, which remains in soft focus even under a magnifying glass: black accents, dark brushed tracks, score the delicate coloured spots and highly subtle background matter, in which emerge a number of red areas. The vision is anguished, despite the title, which suggests the lightness of takeoff. This dialogue between destruction and construction on the pictorial surface is a highly accurate reflection of Wols' tormented soul. In painting, photography and poetry in painting, the artist explores "that very small world (butterfly, horse, cockroach, violin, etc.) that he suffers from within and which inflicts sleep-walking on him." (J-P Sartre)

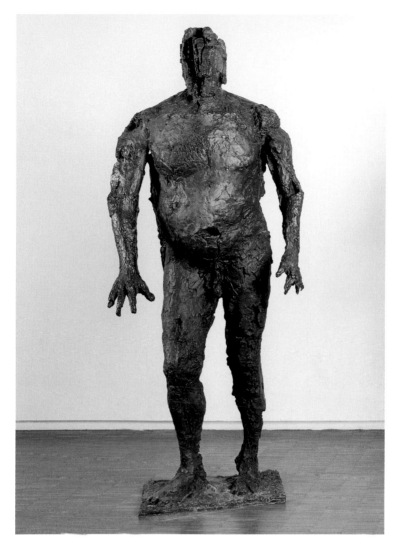

Germaine Richier

1904, Grans (France)
1959, Montpellier (France)

The Storm, 1947-1948
Bronze, 200 x 80 x 52 cm
Purchased in 1949
AM 887 S

Germaine Richier stands out as one of France's great 20th-century sculptors after the end of World War II. However, all her important work was done in a short period, from 1945-1959. A long period of gestation preceded it, the end result of it being a quasi-Expressionist view of the human body.

The Storm, which has a female counterpart called *The Hurricane*, is the embodiment of a natural raw force from which all aestheticism is banished: it thus suggests a link between human flesh and "pieces of bark, rocks, botanical or geographical facts" (J Dubuffet).

Carlo Mollino

1905, Turin (Italy) – 1973, Turin (Italy)

Desk, 1950

Plywood, glass, wood, 78 x 205 x 94 cm
Purchased in 1998
AM 1998-1-3

The Italian designer started his
career with the interior design
of houses, where he designed the
furniture and biomorphic features,
which he provided by the unit.
In the 1950s, he became interested
in moulded plywood, a material
that follows the design most closely
and lends furniture the animality
its creator was looking for. With this
desk, which is both light and firmly
anchored, Mollino goes to extreme
lengths to find a balance in a hollow
structure. On the right, the drawer
case reinforces this impression
because, despite its mass, it seems
suspended in a void. The clear
glass top, almost a simple line,
is apparently inspired by a drawing
of a woman in rear view by Léonor
Fini.

Antoine Pevsner
[Nathan Abramovich Pevsner]

1884, Klimovichi (Russia) – 1962, Paris (France)

World, 1947
Patinated brass rods, 75 x 60 x 57 cm
Gift of Mme Pevsner, 1964
AM 1422 S

Antoine Pevsner produced paintings in a geometric style and constructions in transparent materials before moving on to working with fine strips of metal soldered together. *World*, which dates from the latter period, has a special position in the artist's oeuvre. Contrary to his normal practice, he did a maquette and preparatory drawings first. The metal threads of solder in *World* constitute broad surfaces, which Pevsner afterwards tangled up to get an effect of continuity. Oxidised and coated, they reveal the glints and shadows of their curves to the light. *World* is the image of a universe focused on itself and opening on to its own space.

Jesús Rafael Soto
1923, Ciudad Bolivar (Venezuela)

Rotation, 1952
Oil on plywood, 100.5 x 100 x 7.5 cm
Purchased in 1980
AM 1980-529

Venezuelan artist Jesús-Rafael Soto arrived in Paris in 1950. At the time, he was fascinated by the Bauhaus artists, and Mondrian and Malevich. One year later, he exhibited at the Nouvelles Réalités salon, where he met Tinguely and Agam. In 1955, he exhibited jointly with them at the 'Mouvement' exhibition put on by the Denise René Gallery. Kinetic Art was born, and Soto would become one of its leading lights.

Rotation is among the earliest of the artist's works. It is one of a series of 'repetitions' that established the artist's creative system. The picture is composed like a random musical score, where the alternating juxtaposition of squares and lines produces the illusion of a gyratory movement.

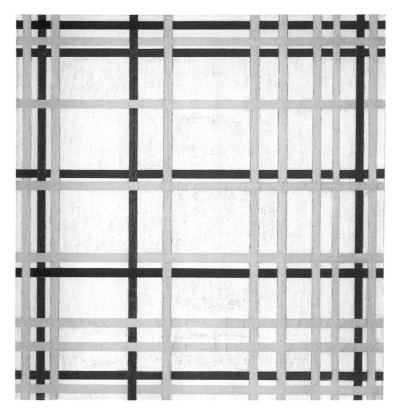

Piet Mondrian

1872, Amersfoort (Netherlands) –
1944, New York (USA)

New York City 1, 1942

Oil on canvas, 119.3 x 114.2 cm
Purchased with the assistance of the
Scaler Foundation, 1984
AM 1984-352

Mondrian travelled a long way not
just geographically when he left
Paris for New York, because the
contrasts, vitality and jazz that mark
life in Manhattan intrigued him. The
austere style of the Parisian years
and asceticism of his Neo-Plasticist
period gave way to the rhythm and
light of his strips of colour (painted
or traced with the help of adhesive
tape), whose geometry revels in a
"pure, unadulterated vitality." Even
so, it did not budge Mondrian from
his conviction that "art will disappear
as life gains greater balance ... We
shan't need paintings and sculptures
any more because we shall be living
in the middle of finished art." He
died not long after, in February 1944.

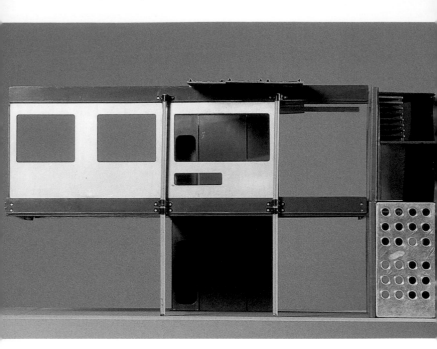

Jean Prouvé

1901, Paris (France) – 1984, Nancy (France)

Industrialised building, 1951

Architect's model of a bay
Metal and wood, 90 x 130 x 90 cm
Held in trust for the Prouvé family
AM 1992-1-dép(27)

Jean Prouvé was more a structural engineer than an architect, with his whole career focused on producing pre-fabricated houses, furniture and structures. This involved techniques he used to construct a flying club at Buc, the Maison du Peuple at Clichy, and 800 homes for disaster victims in Lorraine and the Vosges after the war. Preoccupied with the subject of industrialised building, his starting principle was that a building needed to be constructed with as few components as possible, each having a well-defined structural role, which allowed an organic whole to be developed. This project never saw the light of day.

Le Corbusier
(Charles-Édouard Janneret)

1887, La Chaux-de-Fonds (Switzerland) –
1965, Roquebrune-Cap-Martin (France)

Residential unit, Tiergarten, Berlin,
1957-1958

Model
Wood and various materials
45 x 90 x 122 cm
Purchased in 1994
AM 1994 1 1

Charles-Édouard Jeanneret (Le Corbusier) is both the most famous
and the most underrated architect
of the 20th century. Following
a number of study trips, he settled
in Paris in 1917. Anxious to integrate
into a society devoted to mechan-
isation, he soon developed a func-
tionalist style linked to the artistic
currents of the day. The buildings
he created range from a church
in France to administrative buildings
in India.

In 1956, he was invited by the
City of Berlin to construct a residential unit. As in Marseilles and
Rezé-les-Nantes, it was to house
400 families living independently.
The Berlin project got furthest, but
Le Corbusier's instructions were
disregarded, which provoked his
wrath and doomed the building to
premature decay.

Alexander Calder

1898, Philadelphia (USA) –
1976, New York (USA)

Mobile on two planes, c. 1955
Painted aluminium sheet and steel wires
200 x 120 x 110 cm
Gift of the artist, 1966
AM 1514 S

An artist at the interface of movement and sculpture, lightness and immobility, Alexander Calder, from the 1950s, created mobiles whose triangular components evoke vegetal forms, while the primary colours and black and white are a response to solely three-dimensional requirements. Taking advantage of the laws of equilibrium and the spatial setting, this work is one of a number of air-operated mobiles that move thanks to the metal wings offering resistance to currents of air.

The idea of exploring the possibilities of movement in sculpture arose out of a meeting with Mondrian in the 1930s. An engineer by training, Calder was familiar with the laws of mechanics, and developed ingenious models involving movement, using all sorts of different materials.

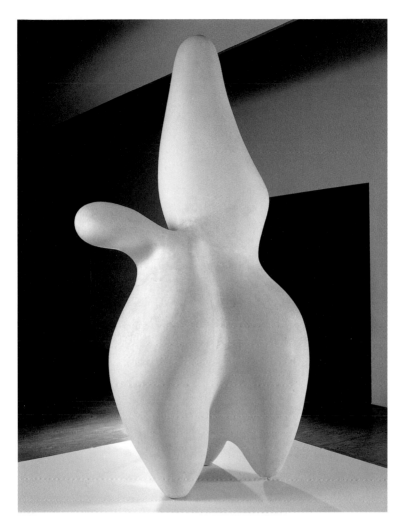

Hans (Jean) Arp

1886, Strasbourg (France)
1966, Basle (Switzerland)

Cloud Shepherd, 1953

Plaster, 320 x 123 x 220 cm
Gift of the artist, 1963
AM 1344 S

Hans Arp, who had both French
and German nationality – Strasbourg was part of German Alsace
at the time of his birth – likewise
belonged to both Zurich Dadaism
and the Parisian avantgarde. A friend
of Tzara, Ernst and Schwitters, he
and his wife, Swiss artist Sophie
Taeuber, settled at Meudon in 1929.

He himself called his explorations
blending abstraction and surrealism
'concrete art.' From 1933, he began
producing his first sculptures in the
round (which stand), in contrast to
his reliefs in wood (which hang).

Cloud Shepherd is one of these
pieces of concrete art, with which
Arp was reviving naturalistic statu-
ary. It is an organic sculpture in
the round, a soft form, an anthropomorphic sculpture that offsets
the rigour of the abstract pieces.
It evokes a bud, a flower, a living
membrane.

Henri Matisse

1869, Le Cateau-Cambrésis (France) –
1954, Nice (France)

Jazz, 1947

Illustrated book with 20 prints of
Matisse collages (incl. 5 full-page prints)
Éditions Tériade, Paris
164 pp; 42.2 x 32.5 cm
250 copies published on Vélin d'Arches
Documentation section, MNAM-CCI

Published with great care as
a bibliophile edition by Tériade
in 1947, *Jazz* was created between
1943 and 1946. This book is the
first important work by Matisse
from cutouts of gouache-painted
paper, a technique he used
during the last decade of his
life and which he considered
a success since "instead of
drawing the outline and filling
it with colour – one modifying
the other – [he] drew directly in
the colour." The idea of writing
a text himself and reproducing
pages of it in facsimile came to
him only in 1946.

Henri Matisse

1869, Le Cateau-Cambrésis (France) –
1954, Nice (France)

The Sorrows of the King, 1952

Cutouts of gouache-painted paper
mounted on canvas, 292 x 386 cm
Purchased in 1954
AM 3279 P

This picture, possibly of biblical
inspiration, is an old man's nostalgic
look at the things he loved – music,
dance and poetry, which are recurrent themes in Matisse's oeuvre.
You can make out the figure of an
elderly king stooping over his
guitar, playing for a young female
dancer dressed in white. Though
the latter is caught in a movement
that carries her towards the edge
of the picture, she nevertheless
leans affectionately towards the
central figure at the same time.
Here, the artist attains the apogee
of his mastery of the technique of
gouache cutouts – sheets previously
covered with colour which he
cut out and placed on the support
once he had decided where to put
the pieces.

Raymond Hains and
Jacques Mahé de la Villeglé

1926, Saint-Brieuc (France) and
1926, Quimper (France)

Ach Alma Manetro, 1949

Torn posters stuck on paper
and mounted on canvas, 58 x 256 cm
Purchased in 1987
AM 1987-938

Raymond Hains and Jacques de
la Villeglé met at the fine arts college
in Rennes, in 1945. From 1950,
they began to collaborate much
more closely, making *décollages*
from posters, photography and film.
Their first joint exhibition took place
in 1957.

Ach Alma Manetro, a joint work
made from posters peeled off and
torn up, is their 'Bayeux tapestry,'
and dates from 1949. The work is
the result of tearing by thousands
of anonymous hands, and to which
the artist adds nothing of its/his
composition. There is no question
of a creative process, just invention.
According to Villeglé, who used the
process throughout his career, the
artist is a collector here.

Willem De Kooning ▲

1904, Rotterdam (Netherlands) –
1997, East Hampton (USA)

Woman, c. 1952

Charcoal and pastel on two papers
pasted on paper, 74 x 50 cm
Purchased 1971
AM 1976-946

For Dutch-born American artist
De Kooning, who was close to Léger
and Picasso, drawing is intimately
bound up with painting. "I draw
when I'm painting, and I don't know
the difference between painting
and drawing." This coloured sketch
is thus part of the famous series of
Women paintings begun in the early
1950s. Violent chromaticism, expres-
sive vigour of line, disproportionate
and grotesque corporeal morphology
are what characterise these 'idols.'
Shapes are suggested by thick charcoal lines blurred by being covered
up, cutouts and transfers show that
destruction is just as much a creator
of forms. Here, the figure cut in two
and put together again leaves a gap
which, having become a linking part
of the drawing, throws doubt on the
figuration.

Sam Francis

1923, San Mateo (USA) –
1994, Santa Monica (USA)

In Lovely Blueness, 1955-1957
Oil on canvas, 300 x 700 cm
Gift of the Scaler Foundation,
with assistance from Sylvie
and Éric Boissonnas, 1977
AM 1977-207

This canvas by Sam Francis is important for more than one reason. Firstly for its size – it is one of the largest Francis painted during his time in Paris, a panoramic format revealing the combined influence of Monet and Matisse. But it also marks a transition in the painter's work. After this, the coloured interwoven cells would explode into clouds, with a more or less precise outline. This canvas is based on a poem by Hölderlin, *In lieblicher Bläue* (which also provided the title): "So simple are the images, so holy / That sometimes one is in truth afraid / To describe them, here in this place."

Jackson Pollock ➤

1912, Cody (USA) –
1956, Southampton (USA)

The Deep, 1953
Enamel and metallic paint on canvas
220.4 x 150.2 cm
Gift of the children of Jean de Menil
and the Menil Foundation, 1976
AM 1976-1230

In 1951, Jackson Pollock temporarily interrupted the production of dripping paintings, abstract pictures projected on the canvas with a stick in a dripping technique, and returned to a technique created five years earlier. He uses a syringe to pour a very liquid black on the white. Shape and background can be made out once more, the dark area opening up a space beyond the surface. The illusion of depth becomes the centre of the canvas, and recalls the doubts that still assailed Pollock at the end of his life regarding his creative process.

Nicolas de Staël

1914, St. Petersburg (Russia) –
1955, Antibes (France)

*The Musicians, in Memory
of Sidney Bechet,* 1953

Oil on canvas, 161.9 x 114.2 cm
Donated in lieu of inheritance tax, 1982
AM 1982-263

Having abandoned abstraction
to explore the ambitious question
of the change between the subjects
of pictures and pictures themselves
as sole subjects, Nicolas de Staël
goes further here in figuration.
The Musicians was inspired by
a concert of Sydney Bechet's that
he attended, and with its broad
vertical layers, bright colours and
strong central emphasis expresses
both the diffuse range of sound
and vibrance of the musical rhythm.
Music played a core role in the life
and work of de Staël, right up to
the last unfinished canvas called
The Concert.

Alberto Giacometti

1901, Stampa (Switzerland) –
1966, Coire (Switzerland)

Venetian Woman V, 1956

Bronze, 110.5 x 31.3 x 14 cm
Donated in lieu of inheritance
tax in 1991
AM 1991-301

From 1945, Alberto
Giacometti began to
create slender, motionless
figures "eroded by the
surrounding space and
light." At first small-scale,
they grew to full-size from
1956. The nine *Venetian
Women* were still three-
quarters size. Among
them, no. 5 seems to be
a transition between two
styles. In the first *Women*,
Giacometti treats his
figures in a single volume.
The same is the case here,
but the head and arms
are now separate from
the trunk. Later, the bodies
would become more
and more elongated, and
details – notably hair –
would begin to appear.

Dado

1933, Cetinje (Yugoslavia/
Montenegro)

Triumph of Death, 1955

Indian inks on paper
40 x 29.2 cm
Donated by
Daniel Cordier, 1983
AM 1983-149

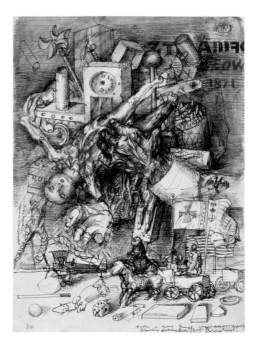

After arriving in Paris in 1956 from his native Yugoslavia, Dado was very soon noticed by Dubuffet, and subsequently by the gallery owner and collector Daniel Cordier. Though scarred by the violence of a world cut in two by the Cold War, Dado nonetheless retained all the freshness of his youthful eye. His first sketches present a vision of a universe deriving from a childhood where horrors and marvels were equally present.

The Triumph of Death is among the first drawings done by Dado before he made the journey to Paris. It brings together a tangle of things: a windmill/airplane propeller, a dice – testimony to the fact that the fate of the world is dedicated by chance – a disembowelled doll and the warlike toys that so expertly stir up children's natural cruelty.

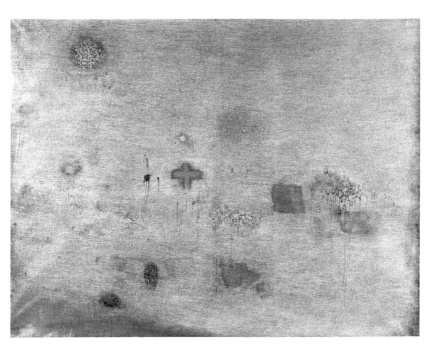

Simon Hantaï

1922, Bia (Hungary)

Painting (Pink Writing), 1958-1959

Coloured inks, gold leaf on linen
329.5 x 424.5 cm
Gift of the artist, 1985
AM 1984-783

♪ Henri Michaux

1899, Namur (Belgium) – 1984, Paris (France)

[Untitled], 1959

Indian ink on paper, 74 x 105 cm
Donated by Daniel Cordier, 1976
AM 1976-1184

In the late 1950s, poet and painter Henri Michaux underwent a series of creative experiences involving taking hallucinogenic substances such as mescaline. Several books were the result, plus a large number of drawings. In these experiments, Michaux was exploring the unknown, boundless, teeming zones of the mind. A novel speed of fluidity with the ink produces a multitude of blobs and lines, sweeping over the whole area of the sheet. These eddies, explosions, migrations, captured in frenetic mid-course, always bring us back to the human dimension, unfolding strange stories and alternative geographies.

Simon Hantaï left Budapest for Paris in 1949. His first experimental works led him to join up with the Surrealists for a time, but he then turned to Abstract Expressionism before developing his folding technique in 1960, which henceforth he stuck to. This work, *Painting (Pink Writing)*, is a key transition work between the two phases, in 1958-59. Littered with the signs (crosses, spots, etc.) already present in his earlier pictures, it is mainly covered with writing that is barely legible, day-by-day copies of texts from the liturgical year and philosophical readings. It is an exceptional work, representing the painter's desire never to stop painting.

Yves Klein

1928, Nice (France) – 1962, Paris (France)

Big Blue Anthropophagy. Homage to
Tennessee Williams (ANT 76), 1960
Pure pigment and synthetic resin on paper
mounted on canvas, 275 x 407 cm
Purchased in 2000
AM 2000-154

"I came up with the idea of painting
with the help of live brushes," is
how Yves Klein, the leading light
of the New Realists, defined in 1961
the process involved in his 'anthro-
pometries,' which he had begun
doing three years earlier. They were
canvases on which women smeared
with blue paint left the prints of their
nude bodies. Less frequently, a kind
of struggle ensued on even larger
canvases, where the disorganised
movements of the body – always
covered in blue, sometimes dragged
or pushed – prevents any discernible
outline arising at all. *Big Blue Anthro-*
pophagy. Homage to Tennessee Williams
shows up particularly well the
powerful vigour of these last an-
thropometries and their impressive
presence.

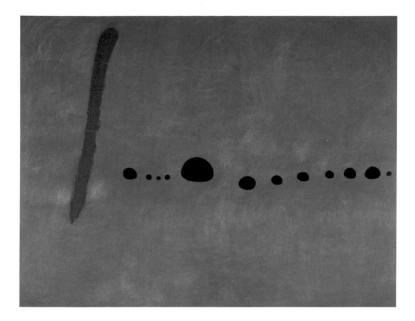

Joan Miró

1893 Barcelona (Spain) –
1983, Palma de Mallorca (Spain)

Blue II, 1961

Oil on canvas, 270 x 355 cm
Gift of the Menil Foundation, 1984
AM 1984-357

This picture is one of a group
of three that Miró hoped could be
reunited. Today, they belong to the
MNAM-CCI, which has a substantial
collection by this artist. Miró worked
on the design of these huge canvases
for a long time, but in the event took
only three months to paint them,
in 1961.

The three pictures are made up
of a blue background, black mineral
elements and a red line that seems to
cross the canvas. The blue is Miró's
"colour of dreams," and evokes his
native Catalonia, but also invites
meditation and reverie. The very act
of painting this background involved
extreme tension for the artist, who
explained: "Completing the background put me in a condition to continue with the rest." As metaphysical
works, the Blues are the result of real
asceticism, and the accomplishment
of Miro's investigations.

Jean Tinguely

1925, Fribourg (Switzerland) –
1991, Berne (Switzerland)

Baluba, 1961-62

Metal, wire, plastic objects, feather duster,
drum, motor; 187 x 5.6.5 x 45 cm
Purchased in 1982
AM 1981-851

Swiss artist Jean Tinguely was
influenced by the Surrealists and
Anarchists. His output includes
astonishing mechanical sculptures,
amongst which are self-destructing
machines. Initially, he was close to
kinetic art, but later joined forces
with the New Realists to create
sculptures from scrap iron with
moving parts. The *Baluba* series is,
like this one, made up of various
materials including wire, plastic
objects, a feather duster, a fuel drum
and an engine. By operating the
pedal attached to it, the viewer sets
off a delightful but disorderly show
that is the 'meaning' of the work.

Tinguely and Niki de Saint-Phalle
were also the creators of the fountain
in the Place Stravinsky, opposite the
Centre Pompidou.

Arman
[Armand Fernandez]
1928, Nice (France)

Home, Sweet Home, 1960

Gas masks in a box
covered with Plexiglass
160 x 140.5 x 20.3 cm
Purchased with assistance from
the Scaler Foundation, 1986
AM 1986-52

From the 1960s, as
a prominent voice of
New Realism, Arman
developed his critique
of a western society con-
demned to consumerism
by piling up rubbish or
used objects, which he
called 'accumulations.'
Such accumulations be-
came the trademark of his contribu-
tion to modern sculpture. Thus *Home,
Sweet Home*, which was acquired for
MNAM-CCI in 1986, is a collection of
gas masks, the repetition of like objects adding a dimension of 'greater
violence,' as Arman put it. The object
chosen – in this case a gas mask –
has, of course, its own message,
as the irony of the title confirms.
But beyond that, the perception the
viewer has of the object and real
things is what matters for the artist.

compression in the form of a parallel-
epiped. In this, the creator anticipates
the effects of operating the press,
and chooses the materials, colours
and arrangement in the machine to
get the end result he wants.

A different industrial process
enabled César's work to develop
into *Expansions*, though still involving the imaginative use of classical
materials such as bronze.

César [César Baldaccini] ➤
1921, Marseilles (France) –
1998, Paris (France)

Compression 'Ricard,' 1962

Controlled compression of a car
153 x 73 x 65 cm
Gift of Pierre Restany, 1968
AM 1968 S

A shortage of money after the war
prompted César to create sculpture
from salvaged objects which he
welded together. Anthropomorphic
or zoömorphic, the works from this
period bear sharp, humorous witness to a society in the process of
reconstruction. With *Ricard*, César
embarked on a new phase of
production involving controlled

Étienne-Martin

1913, Loriol-sur-Drôme (France) –
1995, Paris (France)

The Coat (Dwelling 5), 1962
Various materials, 250 x 230 x 75 cm
Purchased in 1973
AM 1976-965

Étienne-Martin did not belong
to any movement, preferring to
protect his freedom of expression.
He was quite happy to combine
figurative and non-figurative
elements, abstract and concrete.
The *Dwellings* is a series of
works creating sculptural spaces
based on his own experience
in his childhood home. Thus,
number 5, *The Coat*, is more of
a protective suit of armour than
a garment. It is in fact a 'total living
space' made in the image of his
creator. That is perhaps why it is
made up of a collection of found
materials that drive you into a corner
as much as they prompt nostalgia.

the artist "a total bankruptcy of
individuality, owing to masculine
inadequacy in failing to exercise
real responsibilities," a situation
conducive to matriarchy. Erect and
haggard like a ghost, monumental
and stiff like an enormous doll, this
Bride looks like the public prosecutor
of the female condition.

Niki de Saint-Phalle and Jean
Tinguely were joint creators of the
fountain in the Place Stravinsky,
opposite the Centre Pompidou.

Niki de Saint-Phalle ▲

1930, Neuilly-sur-Seine (France)

The Bride, 1963
Wire mesh, plaster, glued lace, various
painted toys; 222 x 200 x 100 cm
Purchased in 1967
AM 1976-1016

In the 1950s, the things that interested her were Art brut, the
Italian and Spanish primitives,
and Gaudí. Subsequently, she
met Tinguely and Klein, and
started doing 'actions,' using
assemblages of plaster filled
with liquid colour which she
fired at with a rifle. The next
phase was her *Nanas*, brightly
coloured sculptures of deformed
women that exorcised ancient
traumas for her.

The Bride, completely white,
and already announcing her suc-
cessors, represents, according to

Martial Raysse

1936, Vallauris (France)

Made in Japan –
La Grande Odalisque, 1964

Acrylic paint, glass, patch,
on a photo mounted on canvas
130 x 97 cm
Gift of the Scaler
Foundation, 1995
AM 1995-213

French artist Martial
Raysse became involved
with the New Realist
and European Pop art
movements while very
young, and he is often
considered the most
brilliant exponent of
the latter. *Made in Japan –*
La Grande Odalisque
belongs to a series
of works containing
quotations from famous
masterworks of painting,
in this case Ingres'
La Grande Odalisque. The pastiche
and use of cheap materials to paint
it, indeed, the first part of the title,
are indicative of the kitsch vision
that Pop art offered. But quotation
works of this kind, where the drawing and colours clash, summon up
a different conflict, one such as the
classicists saw, between reason and
passion.

William Klein ➤

1928, New York (USA)

Pistol 1, New York, 1955
Gelatin silver print, 50.3 x 40.4 cm
Purchased in 1984
AM 1986-215

The work of the American photographer William Klein is as unusual
as it is prolific. Similar to photo-
reportage and fashion photography,
it has nonetheless abundant style,
making every picture a composition,
often cropped, with strong contrasts.
His work has inspired numerous
photographers.

Along with Rome, Moscow and
Tokyo, New York was one of the
cities that Klein roamed with his re-
lentless lens, in each case capturing
the character of the people who live
there. Here, the artist reveals the
obscenity and violence of a situation
where the threatening act by a child
levelling the barrel of a gun at the
photographer – and viewer –
commands the admiration, indeed
near-devotion, of another child.

Yayoï Kusama

1929, Matsumoto (Japan)

My Flower Bed, 1962

Bed springs and painted cotton gloves
250 x 250 x 250 cm
Purchased in 1994
AM 1994-292

Obsessed with images of war and a victim of hallucinations, Yayoï Kusama endeavoured to exorcise her demons through her work. Gouache, water colour and acrylic paint were the means she used to tell of her mental universe. International recognition came overnight. From 1959, she set up installations made of nets and dots like curtains that she placed between herself and other humans. With *My Flower Bed*, Kusama provides another kind of dream environment, as much a crimson flower as the bloody entrails of a man or beast. In order to continue to create and learn to throw off her obsessions, Kusama has lived as a recluse in a Japanese psychiatric institution since 1977.

Robert Rauschenberg ▼

1925, Port Arthur (USA)

Oracle, 1962-1965

Galvanised sheet metal, water and sound effects; 236 x 450 x 400 cm
Gift of Mr and Mrs Pierre Schlumberger, 1976
AM 1976-591

Following the example of his 'combine paintings'– mixing painting and sculpture – Rauschenberg creates here an environment of mutant objects with a radio receiver inside each component picking up broadcasts from all over Europe. In his works, he puts together images of mass culture and objects from everyday life to make fun of their value as icons. A forerunner of Pop art, Rauschenberg succeeded in remaining independent of all movements, making incompleteness the foundation of the process of creation.

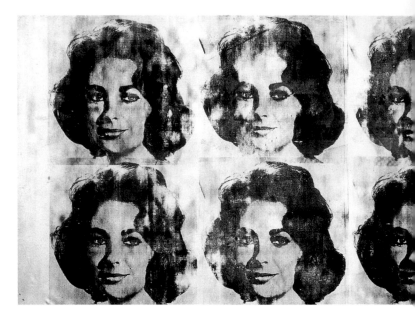

Andy Warhol

1928, Pittsburgh (USA) –
1987, New York (USA)

Ten Lizes, 1963

Oil and varnish on canvas, 201 x 564.5 cm
Purchased in 1986
AM 1986-82

Andy Warhol was both a critic and
a fervent herald of the consumer
society. A scion of Slovak immigrants,
he created a system of production
in which the work of art integrates
the laws of the market, with the role
of the artist becoming outmoded.
His career from the 1960s embraced
silk-screen printing (*Campbell Soups,
Marilyn, Electric Chair,* etc.), the large
output of his Factory workshops,
where the development of other
people's talents (Bob Wilson, etc.)
was encouraged, collaboration with
Velvet Underground, press activities
(*Interview*) and film-making (over
100 films). Warhol was, in fact,
everything that the society of over-
consumption allowed him to be.

Ten Lizes [reproducing the face
of film star Elizabeth Taylor] is one
of the works that best explores the
notion of multiples. The same subject
is reproduced ten times, but imper-
fectly, which gives the canvas
the uniqueness that Warhol had
[apparently] given up.

Chris Marker [Christian-François Bouche-Villeneuve] ▲

1921, Neuilly-sur-Seine (France)

The Pier [The Jetty?], 1962

B/w 35mm film, with soundtrack
Duration: 29 mins.
Purchased in 1999
AM 1999-F 1409

Chris Marker explores all aspects
of memory, using film, video and
multimedia. He has directed several
myth-based films, including this
one, which inspired many artists,
notably John Gillian in his production *L'Armée des douze singes*
[The Army of Twelve Monkeys].
This 29-minute film is made up
entirely of static images in black
and white with a voice off telling
the story. It is a fascinating tale
where past, present and future
mingle and contradict each other
in the mind of a man obsessed with
a childhood memory, the vision of
his own death.

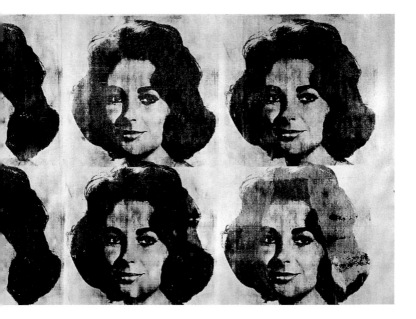

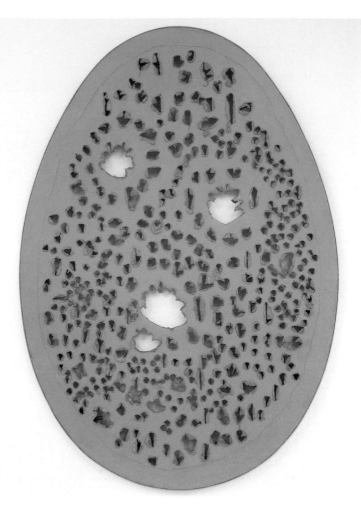

Lucio Fontana

1899, Rosario (Argentina) –
1968, Comabbio (Italy)

The End of God, 1963-64
Oil on canvas, perforations and drawing
178 x 123 cm
Donated in lieu of inheritance tax, 1997
AM 1997-94

Lucio Fontana's youth was spent
partly in Argentina, where he was
born, and Italy, where his family
came from and where he had his
first one-man show in 1930. After
the war, he set out the principles
for a 'spatialist art,' aiming to merge
painting and sculpture, with a view
to challenging the very function
of art.

In 1963-1964, Fontana did one
of his last pictorial series, the *End
of God,* which are among his masterworks. They are 38 monochrome,
oval pictures of identical size pierced
with perforations. They are eggs
with holes, a perfect shape that has
been destabilised and which embody
sacred space.

Mark Rothko [Marcus Rothkowitz]

1903, Dvinsk (Russia) –
1970, New York (USA)

No. 14 (Browns over Dark), 1963

Oil and acrylic on canvas, 228.5 x 176 cm
Purchased in 1968
AM 1976-1015

From 1947, Mark Rothko devoted himself to 'multiforms,' where the colours seem to float on the surface of the canvas. Then in 1950, he came up with the notion of 'ground colour,' solid rectangles of colour super-imposed on a background. Following the example of other artists of American Abstract Expressionism, such as Barnett Newman and Clyfford Still, he asserted the principles of 'colour fields,' which minimise the role of form and brushwork in favour of colour. In *No. 14 (Browns over Dark)*, bright tones have given way to more muted tones of the super-imposed, floating rectangles. *No. 14* seems to be looking to control emotion, and its chiaroscuro is an invitation to sombre but calm meditation.

Bram van Velde

1895, Zoeterwoude (Netherlands) –
1981, Grimaud (France)

[Untitled], 1965
Oil on canvas, 199.5 x 250.5 cm
Purchased in 1982
AM 1982-139

The work of Bram van Velde exists
outside all chronology, because it
is organised like a huge palimpsest.
His canvases are simple surfaces,
or 'expanses' as Beckett called them,
where forms are diluted of their
own accord. Painting excludes
drawing; a structure drawn on the
black wash is progressively covered
over with 'veils' of superimposed
opaque gouache. Rejecting all psycho-
logical preparation, all existential
definition, all production work, all
desire to succeed or fail, Bram van
Velde asserts that painting is the
action of "going and looking, going
to the sight."

Francis Bacon

1909, Dublin (Ireland) – 1992, Madrid (Spain)

Three Figures in a Room, 1964
Oil on canvas, 198 x 441 cm
Purchased in 1968
AM 1976-925

Everything in this triptych suggests that it involves a single scene: the three people are on the same platform; the person in the middle balances the canvas, while the two others seem to be attracted towards the outside. In fact, Bacon has shown the same person in a succession of situations. *Three Figures in a Room* is a kind of retable with a profane trinity. The muted tones and simplicity of décor reinforce the impression of violence and torment issuing from the body, "a flesh and blood order of reality," as the French writer Michel Leiris described it.

Marcel Broodthaers

1924, Saint-Gilles (Belgium)
– 1976, Cologne (Germany)

The Fox and the Crow,
1968

Silk screen printing
on canvas, typewriter
and three silk screen prints
112.4 x 82 x 41 cm
Purchased in 1985
AM 1985-188

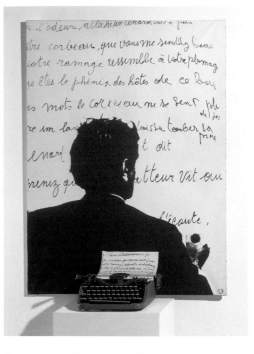

Trained in the Surreal-
ist environment of
wartime and postwar
Brussels, Marcel
Broodthaers saw exhi-
bitions and museums
as a means to subvert
the notion of art and
works of art. He began
by publishing collec-
tions of poems, then
produced a film and
designed object-works.
Throughout his career,
he constantly com-
bined these different vehicles or
modes of expression. Thus, *The Fox
and the Crow* of 1967 is a blend of
a film and a text written on a canvas
serving as a projection screen. He
continued his exploration of the
place of art and the work of art in
museums by creating environments
composed of objects, signs and
figures.

Nam June Paik ▾

1932, Seoul (Korea)

The Moon is the Oldest TV, 1965/1992

11 b/w television sets
Purchased in 1985
AM 1985-142

Nam June Paik is one of the pioneers
of video as an artistic medium. *The
Moon is the Oldest TV,* an ongoing
work from the 1960s to the present
time, was also one of the first in
the medium. Eleven television sets

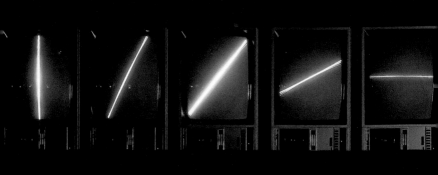

installed in a dark room present the phases of the lunar cycle. A magnet connected to the cathode ray tube modifies the image as the magnetic field changes. The images that result from this intervention reflect a certain Zen philosophy.

Joseph Beuys ▲

1921, Cleves (Germany) –
1986, Düsseldorf (Germany)

*Homogeneous Infiltration
for Grand Piano*, 1966

Piano covered with felt and fabrics
100 x 152 x 240 cm
Purchased in 1976
AM 1976-7

German artist Joseph Beuys was a controversial but key figure of the second half of the 20th century who had great influence on many artists. His work was religiously inspired, particularly by shamanism, and was associated with the Fluxus group and its happenings. It developed around an exploration of death and resurrection, the laws of energy that govern life and the scientific relationships that can be established with them.

Homogeneous Infiltration for Grand Piano, created during an event at the Academy of Fine Arts in Düsseldorf in 1966 describes, according to the artist, the "nature and structure of felt, the piano thus becoming a deposit of sound whose potential filters through the felt." In the early 1980s, Beuys replaced the felt wrapping, thereby creating from it a new work called *The Skin*, which is often present beside the piano. The ensemble is thus consistent with the respect that Beuys had for the evolution of beings and materials.

Jean Dubuffet

1901, Le Havre (France) –
1985, Paris (France)

Winter Garden, 1968-1970
Polyurethane on epoxy resin
480 x 960 x 550 cm
Purchased in 1973
AM 1977-251

Like all constructions by Dubuffet,
the *Winter Garden* is a painting in
three dimensions reflecting a mental
image that has escaped into reality.
The strange universe that issues from
it is unstable, in perpetual expansion
and deceptive (uneven floor, black
lines that follow the contours or
contradict them). It belongs to
a period of creation that Dubuffet
called Hourloupe. Here, in this
enclosed place that the visitor enters,
time, space and the perception of
things, indeed their very reality, are
challenged. The mind loses its bearings and trips up on its own logic.

Mario Merz ◄

1925, Milan (Italy)

Giap's Igloo, 1968
Iron frame, plastic bags filled with earth,
neon tubes, batteries, accumulators
height 120 cm, diam. 200 cm
Purchased in 1982
AM 1982-334

Igloos are a recurrent shape in the
work of Italian artist Mario Merz,
the high priest of Arte Povera.
They turn up in the 1960s in various
guises, made of metal, glass or, like
this one, earth. This work consists
of a metal hemisphere covered with
small bags of earth encircled by
a sentence in neon. Merz wanted
to throw off painting and, for him,
igloos represented the very essence
of an organic shape – the globe and
a shelter. The image of the necessity
of surviving is reinforced here by
a Buddhist-inspired sentence by the
Vietnamese general Giap: "If the
enemy concentrates, he loses ground;
if he disperses, he loses strength."

Giuseppe Penone

1947, Garessio (Italy)

Breath 6, 1978

Terracotta, 158 x 75 x 79 cm
Purchased in 1980
AM 1980-42

A representative of Arte Povera, Giuseppe Penone was both sensitive to the industrial development of north Italy, where he lived, and close to the universe of Virgil and Petrarch. He thus developed an oeuvre where nature and culture shed reciprocal light on each other. It is also an exploration of the completeness of the world, where opposites meet.

   Breath 6 is a terracotta jar made up of three superimposed parts in the dimensions of the imprint left by artist's body. Imprinting life in a receptacle intended for storage, the sculptor's effort is directed towards creating a physical relationship between him and the work.

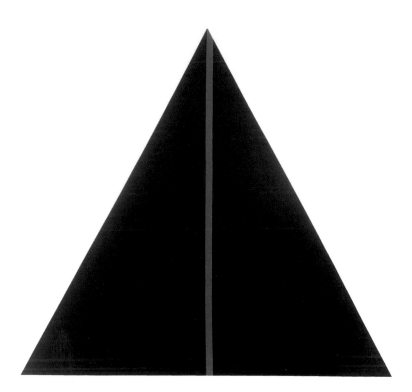

Barnett Newman

1905, New York (USA) –
1970, New York (USA)

Jericho, 1968-1969

Acrylic on canvas, 268.5 x 286 cm
Purchased with the assistance
of Élisa and Basile Goulandris, 1986
AM 1986-272

From 1946, breaking with his previous attachment to automatism stemming from his early Surrealist connections, American painter Barnett Newman succeeded in radically simplifying his pictorial style. Considering the surface of the canvas as initially defined by its internal and external structuring, he chose to construct his paintings using vertical strips (called 'zips') demarcating intensely coloured fields. Newman's organisation of paintings highlights the essential components of his pictures – the format (quite exceptionally by normal standards, a triangle), the colour saturation of the surface, and the subtle internal balance of the work (defined by an off-centre zip).

As such, the work and its title draw the viewer into meditative contemplation about the sublime essence of art.

Eva Hesse

1936, Hamburg (Germany) –
1970, New York (USA)

Seven Poles, 1970

Aluminium wires, polyethylene,
fibreglass, resin; 272 x 240 cm
(variable, depending on the space)
Purchased in 1986
AM 1986-248

On a trip to Germany in 1965, German-born American artist Eva Hesse began a series of drawings of human organs and reliefs made from industrial scrap. On her return to New York, she created sculptures using these as inspiration, producing biomorphic forms made of latex foam, resin or fibreglass.

Seven Poles – dated 1970, the year of her death – is her last work. It brings together seven elements suspended from the ceiling and rest-ing lightly on the floor. It recalls the shape and texture of entrails, but could equally have been inspired by a group of Olmec figurines, the artist already having been influenced in other works by sculptures of this type.

Donald Judd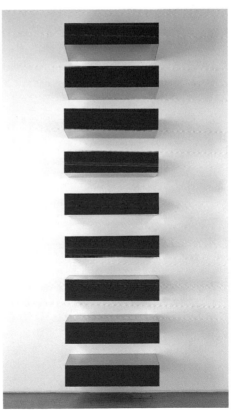

1928, Excelsior Springs (USA) – 1994, New York (USA)

Stack, 1972
Stainless steel and Plexiglass
470 x 102.5 x 79.2 cm;
each component:
23 x 101.6 x 78.7 cm
Purchased in 1973
AM 1980 412

Stack is what Donald Judd called a 'specific object.' Ten industrially made parallelepipeds are stacked up for the full height of the wall at regular intervals. This work, symmetrical and repetitive, forestalls any narration or subjective expression. It belongs to a series of arrangements and progressions produced from 1966, in which all that changed was the size, the material, the number of components and the colour. Henceforth, with this game of variations, the work of art has no longer reference to anything except itself. It represents one of the best examples of minimal art.

Claes Oldenburg

1929, Stockholm (Sweden)

'Ghost' Drum Set, 1972

10 components in
painted sewn canvas,
polystyrene blocks
80 x 183 x 183 cm
Gift of the Menil
Foundation, 1975
AM 1975-64

Swedish-born
American artist
Claes Oldenburg
occupies a special
position in Pop art.
From 1965, he began to
use everyday objects in his
work that he presented devoid of
their essence and colour. Removed
from their contexts, these ghosts thus
become a statement about reality.

Here, he reproduces an orchestral
set out of scale – a memory of a
drum he bought as an adolescent –
in a soft shape without reality and
spectral in its pallor. "The *Drum Set*
is more of a landscape than an object,"
says Oldenburg, "a kind of Brue-
ghelian panorama." The artist is thus
perhaps evoking the snow-capped
peaks of Colorado, a reminder that
he creates monumental works for
installation in the heart of cities.

of the Union des artistes modernes.
He began to design chairs from 1945,
but it was not until the early 1960s
that his genius became evident
when he and Verner Panton became
one of the leading exponents of the
soft, coloured style typical of the
period. Fascinated by the sculptural
opportunities offered by synthetic
materials (latex foam, reinforced
polyester), he created a large number
of chairs, like this *Ribbon Chair 582* –
a knotted ribbon, hollow in the
centre, a place to relax which is both
broad and roomy, with the separate
base acting as a pedestal.

Pierre Paulin

1927, Paris (France)

Ribbon Chair 582, 1966

Steel, lacquered wood,
latex foam
70 x 105 x 80 cm
Gift of Strafor, 1996
AM 1996-1-3

French designer Pierre
Paulin initially trained
in ceramics at Vallauris
and sculpture at Beaune
before joining the
Camondo school and,
subsequently, the studio
of Marcel Gascoin, a
young interior designer

Superstudio

Adolfo Natalini,
1941, Pistoia (Italy)
Cristiano Toraldo di Francia,
1941, Florence (Italy)
Roberto Magris,
1935, Florence (Italy)
Gian Piero Frassinelli,
1939, Porto San Giorgio
(Italy)
Alessandro Magris,
1941, Florence (Italy)

Monumento Continuo,
New New York, 1969

Colour photomontage
Purchased in 2000
AM 2000-2-105

Adolfo Natalini and Cristiano Toraldo di Francia founded Superstudio in 1966, and were subsequently joined by the other members of the group. As an avant-garde group championing a radical architecture, their twenty years of research are an exceptional example of longevity. In 1969, for example, they invented a three-dimensional structure that traversed towns and nature without disturbing it. This project, *Monumento Continuo*, has similarities to works on the destruction of the architectural object, and thus attacking the functionalists and Le Corbusier, but it is the evocative power of its images that will assure its fame and not its contradictory nature.

In the early 1960s, British architects Warren Chalk, Peter Cook, Dennis Crompton, David Greene, Ron Herron and Michael Webb published *Amazing Archigram*, a manifesto for a new way of life and thought. Following the example of Pop artists, Archigram asserted its aim to be in tune with the times. For nearly ten years, the group would turn out utopistic projects, sometimes borrowing from the Situationists, to propound a self-generating and anarchic architecture, developing its models ad infinitum.

Instant City is a collage by Ron Herron that presents this desire to be free in an exuberant and playful way in order to "transform a weekend retreat into a small city of half a million inhabitants."

Archigram

Peter Cook,
1936, Southend-on-Sea
(England)
Dennis Crompton,
1935, Blackpool (England)
Ron Herron,
1930, London (England) –
1995, London (England)

Instant City,
Urban Action Tune-up,
1969-1970

Collage, 58 x 76 cm
Purchased in 1992
AM 1992-1-285

Ettore Sottsass

1917, Innsbruck (Austria)

Toilets and Shower,
1972
Reinforced polyester
Each part:
214 x 96.5 x 100 cm
Gift of the Scaler
Westbury Foundation,
1999
AM 1998-1-25

Ettore Sottsass
is more interested
in enquiry than
producing. His work
is made to be pre-
sented in a museum
rather than to be
integrated into the
framework of every-
day life. The Italian
designer ponders
upon his time and
the changes it has
witnessed. That is why this collection
of cabins, adjustables and mobiles
was shown in 1972 at MoMA, in New
York. *Container furniture* comprises
a kitchen, library, juke-box, seating,
bathroom, toilets (the latter three
forming part of the MNAM-CCI
collection) – ten prototypes in all,
interconnected at the top for the
fluids and power to circulate and
at the bottom to remove waste. The
layout can be modified as desired,
as simply as you change a shirt.

Renzo Piano, Richard Rogers ◀

1937, Genoa (Italy) and 1933, Florence (Italy)

Centre Georges Pompidou,
Paris (France), 1971-1977
Architectural model
Wood, plastic, lichen, metal; 46 x 150 x 98 cm
Gift of the architects, 1999
AM 1999-2-82

In response to the project for a
national centre of art and culture
launched by President Georges
Pompidou in 1969, young architects
Renzo Piano and Richard Rogers,
associates of the Ove Arup research
consultancy, won the architectural

competition in 1971 presided over
by Jean Prouvé. Occupying only half
the site and opening on to a large
piazza that occupied the other half,
this large building reveals its work-
ings to the world. 138 feet (42m) high
and 525 feet (160m) long, the façade
presents a huge mass of glazing
and repeating framework that recall
the utopistic projects of Sant'Elia,
Cedric Price's Fun Palace or the
'social condensers' of Constructivist
architecture. It was commissioned on
31 January 1977, but was renovated
and partly refurbished, from 1997
to 2000, by Piano and Jean-François
Bodin. A restaurant in the style of the
original architecture by Dominique
Jakob and Brendan McFarlane has
been created on the 6th floor.

Aldo Rossi ➤

1931, Milan (Italy) – 1997, Milan (Italy)

Théâtre du monde, Venice, 1979-1980
Engraving on cardboard
70 x 84.5 cm
Purchased in 1992
AM 1992-1-22

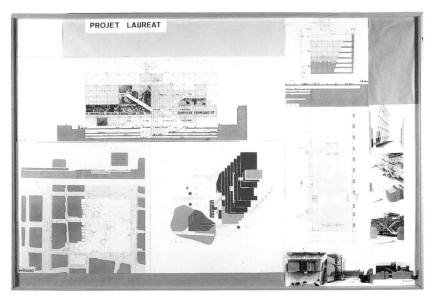

An ephemeral structure, the *Théâtre du monde* floated on Venice's lagoon for several months to accommodate shows of the theatre and architecture section of the Venice Biennale in 1979. 82 feet (25m) high and built to a symmetrical ground plan, the cube shape was crowned by a pointed octagonal prism. The structure was clad in wood and composed of metal tubes fixed to a pontoon.

The stage was surrounded by tiers of seating capable of accommodating 200-250 people. With this structure, Aldo Rossi wanted to evoke Venice as it was prior to stone and marble, a Venice made of wood. But this precarious theatre, both in its brief life and appearance, also raised the issue of disfigured cities, historic centres in peril, in fact, Venice itself.

Pierre Alechinsky ➤
1927, Brussels (Belgium)

The Unnoticed Past, 1981
Acrylic, Indian ink on paper mounted
on canvas; 209 x 470 x 7 cm
Purchased in 1995
AM 1995-339

The Belgian artist Pierre Alechinsky was a member of the Cobra movement from the early 1950s, and his taste for the crossover between painting and literature survives from that time. A great calligrapher, being a specialist in oriental calligraphy, he displays his great mastery of pictorial writing in *The Unnoticed Past*. The use of margins there is characteristic of his work. At the centre are the Gilles (Belgian carnival figures) in colour, and all round, like in the boxes of a comic strip, the minutiae of the different parts of their costumes in black and white.

The collection has acquired a large number of drawings, gouaches and water colours thanks to the artist's generosity.

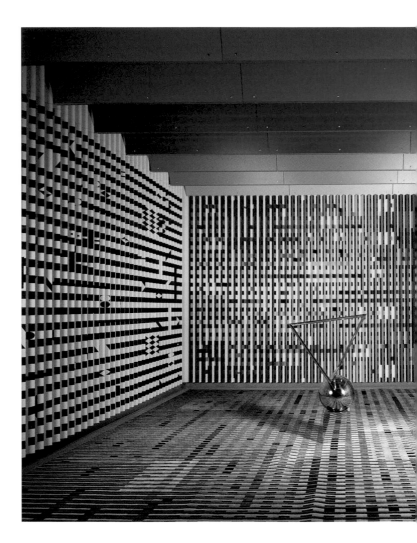

Yacoov Agam [Jacob Gipstein]

1928, Rishon le Zion (Israel)

Salon Agam, 1974

Interior of antechamber to private
apartments of Elysée Palace
for President Georges Pompidou
Various materials
470 x 548 x 622 cm; floor surface 34 m²
Purchased in 1974
AM 2000-3

In the early 1970s, French president
Georges Pompidou decided to have
the private apartments of the presi-
dential palace refurbished by contemporary artists and designers.
Agam designed this antechamber
for him, a kinetic reception room
containing three painted walls,
a coloured, translucent ceiling
and a 194-colour Gobelins carpet.
At the entrance, movable transparent
Plexiglass panels in different colours
progressively modify the tonality of
the room. At the centre of the carpet
is *The Flying Triangle,* a polished steel
sculpture whose distorting reflection
adds still further to this notion of
a fourth dimension. A major work
of kinetic art, Agam's antechamber
creates an unsettling environment
for the head of state's transit from
public to private life.

Bertrand Lavier, François Morellet

1949, Châtillon-sur-Seine (France) and 1926, Cholet (France)

Lavier/Morellet, 1975-1995
Acrylic paint on canvas, 200 x 200 cm
Purchased in 2001
AM 2001-27

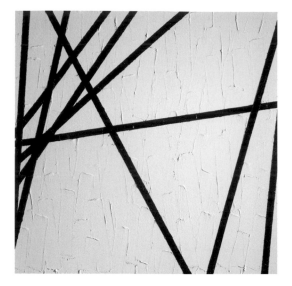

This simple-looking picture becomes complex as soon as you know its story. There are three different versions (only one of which belongs to the MNAM-CCI), successively created by two French artists, François Morellet and Bertrand Lavier.

Morellet was the first to work on the canvas. Sticking to his research into the rules of chance, he drew straight lines linking the letters of the first names of the two artists written on opposite edges of the frames. Lavier subsequently painted over these lines and the space between, using his technical of acrylic painting applied in broad brushstrokes in the style of Van Gogh. This is not a painting but an ambiguous combination, at the junction of picture and painted object.

Pierre Soulages

1919, Rodez (France)

Painting, 1985, 324 x 362 cm, polyptych C, 1985
Oil on canvas, 324 x 362.5 cm
Purchased in 1987
AM 1987-937

Ever since he started painting in the 1950s, Pierre Soulages has remained faithful to an abstract style, constantly exploring a single colour (black) in different ways. Using new formats, taking advantage of unusual contrasts, exploring other techniques (etching and stained glass), Soulages has established an international reputation that puts him in the forefront of French artists of the 20th century.

Painting, 1985, 324 x 362 cm, polyptych C is a collection of four superimposed frames with a succession of broad, black-painted, wrought solids placed obliquely on them. The light catches these hollowed lines of furrows, and the material that is created from this association evokes rain and an enclosing wall alike.

Robert Ryman ➤

1930, Nashville (USA)

Chapter, 1981
Oil on canvas, 4 metal clips
223.5 x 213.5 cm
Purchased in 1982
AM 1981-850

This canvas combines the two fundamental components of Robert Ryman's work: first of all, white, which "enables you to make other things visible" – in this case, sensitivity of material and meticulousness of brushwork are used to make the gesture visible in all its mastery, as well as the infinite variety in the single colour. Secondly, there is the

canvas (a square, as in all of Ryman's works, because in his view that is a perfect shape), placed in front of the wall thanks to a system of fixings that are intentionally visible. Shadows appear around this large-dimensioned canvas, thus doubling the effect of the painted surface.

Bill Viola

1951,
Flushing (USA)

*Chott El-Djerid
(Portrait in
Light and Heat),*
1980

1 videotape,
soundtrack,
colour; screen,
corridor
Duration: 28 mins.
Purchased in 1985
AM 1985-446

American
video artist Bill
Viola reverses the idea and the
reality of a mirage and makes a
subjective truth out of an objective
'lie.' A salt lake in Saharan Tunesia,
Chott el-Djerid is a landscape of
illusions where you can study, in
great heat, people and places that
don't exist. The air there is so hot
it is almost palpable. It acts as a
curtain revealing silhouettes, lorries,
a town, trees, etc. These images
are contrasted with those of grass-
lands in winter, inverse deserts,
which disorientate the viewer just
as much: Viola encourages the
viewer to allow him/herself to
become destabilised by this loss
of bearings and follow this imbalance as if it involved a dream
of his/her own.

Gerhard Richter ➤

1932, Dresden (Germany)

Chinon no. 645, 1987

Oil on canvas, 200 x 320 cm
Purchased in 1988
AM 1988-593

German painter Gerhard Richter
occupies a special position in the history of 20th-century art. He has clearly
shown that he is not to be classified
with either the abstract or the figurative
painters, since he endeavours to go
from one to the other without ever aban-
doning a certain political vision of art.

Chinon no. 645 celebrates landscape
in a time of photography. Without
being hyperrealist, the style forces the
viewer to look at the detail. It is thus
possible to distinguish in the distance
a nuclear power station, which at
a stroke reduces this rural landscape
to desolation. Richter invites us to
think twice: about the dangers of the
post-industrial world and the conven-
tions of style.

Bernd and Hilla Becher

1931, Siegen (Germany) and
1934, Potsdam (Germany)

Blast Furnaces, 1982

Gelatine silver print, 59 x 49 x 2 cm
Purchased in 1992
AM 1991-339(18)

Bernd and Hilla Becher
are among the pioneers
of contemporary German
photography. Masters of a
photographic style distanced
from the subject, they draw
up inventories of pitheads,
water towers, half-timbered
gables, etc. – a wealth of
anonymous sculptures cre-
ated by technical progress or
the evolution of our societies.

The juxtaposition of
18 German, American and
French blast furnaces shows
that these monsters of sheet
metal and steel belong to a single
family far beyond all specific
qualities linked with national

industries. The photographers' eyes
breathes new power into these
abandoned giants, a different raison
d'être.

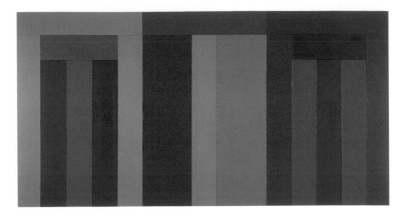

Brice Marden

1938, Bronxville (USA)

Thira, 1979-1980

Oil and wax on canvas, 244 x 460 cm
Gift of the Georges Pompidou
Art and Culture Foundation, 1983
AM 1983-190

Thira is Brice Marden's masterpiece.
American painter Marden was
initially influenced by Franz Kline
and Jasper Johns. The monochromes
that he began to paint from 1964
still show the preparation of the
canvas, which distinguishes him
from the minimalists. From 1968,
his paintings consisted of several
vertical panels, in ever increasing
number, until in *Thira* eighteen
panels are combined, forming
three door frames or three cruci-
fixes. In either case, the topic is
that of passing to the next world
or another dimension, that of a
non-immediate reality.

▼ Jean-Marc Bustamente

1952, Toulouse (France)

T. 21A .79. 1979, 1979

Colour photograph, 103 x 130 cm
Gift of the artist, 2001
AM 2001-31

Since the end of the 1970s, Jean-Marc
Bustamente's oeuvre has comprised
photos, paintings, sculptures and
installations. His first pieces from
1978-1982, photos which he later
called *Tableaux* [Pictures], nicely
illustrate the concept of 'transitional
areas,' a form of indetermination
that he wanted
to bring to his
work.

Like *T. 21A. 79.
1979*, these *Tableaux*
are photos of
Barcelona land-
scapes between
town and country-
side. Landscapes
that disappear
in the examination
of the details, so
that the viewer is
kept at a distance,
on the surface of
the image.

Bruce Nauman

1941, Fort Wayne (USA)

Dream Passage with Four Corridors,
1984
Panels, fluorescent tubes, tables, chairs
283 x 1,241 x 1,241 cm
Purchased in 1987
AM 1987-1136

Defying classification, American
artist Bruce Nauman has an extensive oeuvre to his credit. He creates
pieces using very diverse materials,
sculptures in neon and photographs,
installations using film or sound-
tracks, videos – particularly since
the 1980s. He also writes notes and
drawings for his work.

Dream Passage with Four Corridors
is a large-scale installation made up
of two narrow intersecting corridors
and a central room with chairs and
tables, the whole being lit by yellow
and red neon lights. This work combines the recurrent ideas in Nauman
of transition and balance in space by
the organisation of the neon lights,
the violent impact of their colours
and the reversing and doubling
of different elements.

Mike Kelley, Tony Oursler

1954, Los Angeles (USA) and
1957, New York (USA)

The Poetics Project, 1977-1997

Various materials, 3 sculptures, 14 paintings,
11 videotapes, colour, soundtrack
Gift of the Société des Amis du MNAM,
with the support of the Scaler Westbury
Foundation, 1999
AM 1999-148

In 1977, American West Coast artists
Tony Oursler and Mike Kelley
created a punk group called
The Poetics. This installation,
shown for the first time in 1997,
celebrates memories of that period
based on certain works dating from
the period and new ones added to
complete the ensemble. A research
and multimedia installation project,
The Poetics Project incorporates
paintings, videos, sculptures,
music and drawings. It invites the
visitor to stroll among the different
elements, to look at them as if in-
specting, to listen as if snooping.
Although Kelley and Oursler have
separate careers of their own, the
Poetics Project is a real revelation of
their creative environment.

Ilya Kabakov

1933, Dnepropetrovsk (Ukraine, USSR)

The Ten People: The Man who Flew Away into Space, 1981/1988

Various materials
Approximate dimensions: 280 x 610 x 244 cm
Purchased in 1990
AM 1990-97

The Man who Flew Away into Space is part of a huge piece called *The Ten People* that Soviet artist Kabakov designed, not without humour, on the model of Soviet communal apartments. This installation would allude to those who go out of their way to escape all everyday responsibility, like the avantgarde of the 1920s. While setting up all the archetypes of the Soviet world (the fur hat, propaganda posters, etc.), it also expresses the dream of escaping to another reality – like the conquest of space. Nevertheless, Kabakov always puts the ideology back into the centre of his work. Here, a ghostly figure, a victim of utopia, reproduces the system.

Daniel Buren

1938, Boulogne-Billancourt (France)

Cabin No. 6: Draughtboards, 1985

Wooden frame and striped material
283 x 424.5 x 283 cm
Purchased from the artist in 1990
AM 1990-87

All Daniel Buren's work can be read in alternating 3 ¼″ (8.7 cm) vertical stripes of white and colour, the presentation of which is adapted on the spot by the artist. Using these stripes, he highlights, juxtaposes, emphasises or alternates for contrast the nature of a place or support. With this impersonal motif, Buren aims to develop a personal style, which evolves by the use of different materials (paper, fabric, glass, mirror, plastic, etc.) and moves from plane to volume.

He designed *Exploded Cabin No. 6* by superimposing the plans of two houses constructed side by side by Mies van der Rohe in Krefeld (Germany), thus transposing one house into another. The cutouts of the *Cabins*, projected on to the surrounding walls, force the visitor who stations himself in the middle of them to regard the space around him as another work.

The *Cabins* are works in situ and, therefore, by nature ephemeral, so they are always photographed to record the memory of them.

Toni Grand

1935, Gallargues-le-Montueux (France)

Double Column, 1982

Wood and polyester laminate
Each component: 210 cm, diam.: 80 cm
Purchased in 1983
AM 1983-372

A member of the Supports/Surfaces group, sculptor Toni Grand works on the quality of the materials and their symbolism. Thus, here, he has chosen to make a work in wood and laminate, a natural versus an industrial material, a noble versus an ordinary material. Two columns of double kind combine a found form with a manufactured form. On the outside, the columns present a double appearance: rough and smooth, perfect and imperfect. The interior is hollow to make its space visible. Both fragile and imposing, the *Double Column* retains an air of mystery, like every work by Grand.

Claude Viallat ◄

1936, Nîmes (France)

Homage to Matisse, 1992
Acrylic on canvas
340 x 250 cm
Gift of the artist, 1994
AM 1994-139

Painter of imprints,
Claude Viallat imprints,
draws or paints knuckle-
bone shapes, with which
he covers the canvas.
This motif, carried over
from one work to the
next, transforms each
of them into an image
of the creative process.
A founder member of
the Supports/Surfaces
group, Viallat gave up
using canvases stretched
on frames, sometimes
salvaging various mate-
rials, which he paints
or turns into sculptures.

In the *Homage to
Matisse* series, he asserts
the presence of the
master in his work.
This canvas – of a
parasol – is sub-titled

The Yellow Curtain. It is a reinter-
pretation of a work of the same
name painted by Matisse in 1915.
The 'knucklebones' are framed
by the wavy edges of the canvas
just as in the source work the
curtains frame the window.

Jean Nouvel

1945, Fumel (France)

Tokyo Opera.
Prize-winning
competition
project, 1986

In collaboration with
É. Blamont, J.-M. Ibos,
P. Starck and M. Vitart
Not carried out
Architectural model
Black and gold plastic
55 x 122 x 90 cm
Purchased in 1992
AM 1992-1-381

Jean Nouvel is an ad-
vocate of a critical
architecture that
challenges con-
ventional models
of thinking by inte-
grating the concerns of the times.
His buildings and projects adapt
to their environment, to the point
where they reorganise it to give
a new coherence to the urban fabric.
The design for the Institute of the
Arabic World gave Nouvel a spring-
board to international renown.
A year later, he submitted his opera
project to Tokyo (not carried out),

a 'black monolith' and 'counter-form'
of a piano, an evocation of Japanese
culture disembarking in an SF universe. The three suspended rooms
covered with gold seem to emerge
from the entrails of this massive
musical box, all ready to close on
itself again.

Jean-Pierre Raynaud

1939, Courbevoie (France)

Container Zero, 1988

Steel, tiles, lighting; 330 x 330 x 330 cm
Purchased in 1988
AM 1988-2(1)

▲ Luigi Colani

1928, Berlin (Germany)

Racing motorcycle, 1986

Reinforced polyester, 130 x 260 x 75 cm
Gift of Strator firm, 1992
AM 192-1-413

German designer Luigi Colani
has been famous from the first for
his creations in the motor industry.
Since 1968, he has been interested
in plastic bodywork and has studied
aerodynamics. The creator of bio
morphic machines, such as a yacht
in the form of a whale, he designed
a motorcycle like a springing feline
for Yamaha, one of the last projects
he did in Japan, where he lived from
1982 to 1986. This machine broke
a world speed record in 1986, reach-
ing 210 mph (336 km/h). Colani's
biodesign still inspires countless
designers and has transformed the
vision of their art.

This work was commissioned by
the MNAM-CCI and constitutes
a museum within a museum. Other
works are exhibited in it, either
by Jean-Pierre Raynaud himself
(as here, *Flag 2000*) or artists relating
to his world (Malevich's *[Black] Cross*
of 1915).

    Container Zero picks up the prin-
ciple of a house entirely in ceramic
tiles that Raynaud had had built in
the Paris area. He lived in it, opened
it to the public in 1974 and then
destroyed it in 1988. This is the
space before the work, the moment
before birth. But it is also a place
of asceticism that clinical coldness,
disengagement and blind spots in
the lighting render inaccessible to us.
Inspired by the philosophy of Malevich, Raynaud's world became one
of introspection and meditation.

Cindy Sherman

1941, Glenn Ridge (USA)

Untitled, # 141, 1985
Colour proof on paper
184.2 x 122.8 cm
Purchased in 1986
AM 1986-264

The entire oeuvre of American artist Cindy Sherman is based on ideas about images and how they function, particularly female stereotypes as they come across in films. She uses herself as a subject, working out the setting, adopting and interpreting a new role every time like a prisoner in a picture story without text. Since 1982, her work has taken on a more spectacular dimension. She composes brightly coloured images in which the character or characters appear disabled, burdened with artificial limbs or looking like freaks. This applies to *Untitled, # 141*, where the whole setting, the yellow and black hues of the clothes and the bottom-lit scene evoke a diabolical character.

Sophie Calle

1953, Paris (France)

The Blind: the beautiful I've kissed it goodbye, 1986
Gelatine silver prints, wood, metal
108 x 120 x 15 cm
Gift of the Société des Amis
du MNAM, 1992
AM 1992-368

Inviting people to undergo an experience for which she has defined the rules in advance, Sophie Calle keeps records of the experiment by means of written documentation, photos, recordings, films, etc. The presentation of this documentation is not the work itself but a summary of it; the experiment does not make a complete work without the records that result from it. Thus, for *The Blind*, Sophie Calle asked people blind from birth to describe what beautiful meant to them. The photos of them, their written replies and the very impersonal interpretation that she gives of it are then put on show. One man replied that he had kissed beauty goodbye, and Calle left the shelf empty where she would have placed the image illustrating his reply.

Christian Boltanski

1944, Paris (France)

The C. B. Archives, 1965-1988, 1989
Metal, photographs, lights, electrical wiring
270 x 693 x 35.5 cm
Purchased in 1989
AM 1989-551

Christian Boltanski's output unfolds like the long thread of a traumatised memory. The *C. B. Archives 1965-1988* is an installation consisting of more than 600 metal boxes accumulated

between 1965 and 1988 and intended to conserve the story of Boltanski's life down to the last details, thanks to the 1,200 photos and 800 documents that it contains. Both necessary and pathetic, beneath a row of spotlights, the wall now takes refuge in the sole holy spot in the contemporary world that can assure the immortality of its creator – a museum. Yet, removed from the artist's eye and out of the public's sight, these boxes not only preserve the traces of Christian Boltanski's existence, they obliterate them.

Jean-Luc Godard
1930, Paris (France)

Histoire(s) du Cinéma I to VIII
Toutes les histoires, Une histoire seule,
Seul le cinéma, Fatale beauté,
La Monnaie de l'Absolu, Une vague
nouvelle, Le Contrôle de l'univers,
Les Signes parmi nous, 1989/1996

Videotape, b/w and colour, soundtrack
Duration: 51, 42, 26, 28, 26, 27, 27 and
37 minutes.
Purchased in 2000
AM 2000-172 (1 to 8)

Histoire(s) du Cinéma is a video series
containing eight episodes of an
ambitious project – to bring together
individual stories and history itself.
Godard thus offers an encounter
between his own films and those
that are already part of history,
by means of a montage of texts
and photograms. This work is the
location of a memory constantly
in the making, a cinema historian's
work in progress, being himself
an actor in this history. This unique
venture carries its own myth.
And the visitor to the Museum
can experience it in part.

Louise Bourgeois

1911, Paris (France)

Precious Liquids, 1992

Various materials
472 cm, diam. 442 cm
Purchased in 1993
AM 1993-28

Focused entirely on the life of its creator and in particular her childhood, the work of Louise Bourgeois powerfully (and sometimes terrifyingly) evokes the conflict between her and her father. A major piece, *Precious Liquids* explores all the themes dear to the artist by bringing them together. On the outside of this installation in the shape of a New York water tank is a simple sentence: "Art is the guarantee of mental health." Inside, the visitor discovers a little iron bedstead with a puddle of water and, all around, glass bottles intended to be passed through by blood, urine, sperm, tears – all the precious liquids emitted by the human body and symbols of grief and pleasure. Opposite the bed is an immense man's coat enclosing a child's dress embroidered with the words 'Merci / Mercy,' a bilingual evocation of a feeling of pity and gratitude for the figure of her father.

Gabriel Orozco △

1962, Veracruz (Mexico)

Worktables, 1990-2000
Mixed techniques
Variable dimensions
Purchased in 2001
AM 2001-91

A major figure in contemporary
art, Gabriel Orozco has a highly
individual approach to sculpture,
inspired both by the materials
and concerns of Arte Povera
(Penone, Pistoletto) and the pro-
cessual works of Matta, Clark
and Serra.

These worktables make up a
summary of a decade of his sculptural practice. Everything that
emerged from his studio, models,
drawings, texts, studies for works –
whether carried out or not – heterogeneous and sometimes most
peculiar items such as saliva and
toothpaste, illustrates not only
Orozco's creative process but also
his formal and poetic vocabulary.
The items highlight the extent of
Orozco's intense concern for the
close relationship between sculpture
and the everyday world.

Annette Messager

1943, Berck-sur-Mer (France)

Pikes, 1992-1993
Pikes, pencils, pastel pictures under glass,
objects, fabric, nylon stocking
250 x 800 x 425 cm
(variable, depending on space)
Purchased in 1994
AM 1994-85

Annette Messager asserts her identity as a woman not to espouse
feminist causes, which are too
simplistic, but to focus on the idea
of identity itself. Assuming several
at once, and refusing to choose

a technique, she takes over the
paraphernalia of the domestic
environment to sabotage a world
organised by males.

In *Pikes*, soft toys, stuffed animals
and grotesque beasts, some of which
are shaped into women's stockings,
are impaled on knitting needles
metamorphosed into revolutionary
pikes. Halfway between Perrault
and Kafka, this macabre ritual,
which evokes Mexican festivals,
Halloween or the bloody fervour
of the Terror, remind us that fairy
tales "are terrifying and cruel"
(A. Messager).

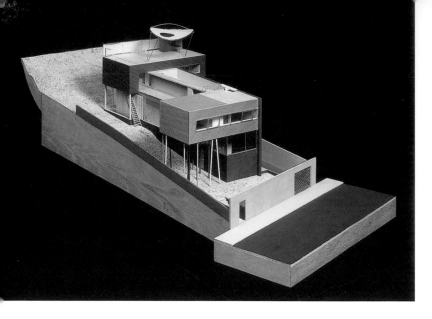

Rem Koolhaas

1944, Rotterdam (Netherlands)

Villa Dall'Ava, 1990-1991

Architectural model
Plastic, wood, cork, paper and metal
41 x 120 x 55 cm
Purchased in 1992
AM 1992-1-40

Rem Koolhaas designed this house in Saint-Cloud for a couple with a child. Built on a sloping site, with a view of the Eiffel Tower and the Bois de Boulogne, it fits in well in this smart suburb of Paris, amidst bourgeois houses and suburban homes.

One may discern in the design a number of quotations from the great moments of 20th-century domestic architecture, such as the piles, façade and interior ramp of Le Corbusier's Villa Savoye, the arrangements of Eileen Gray's villas, Mies van der Rohe's handling of glass and curtains, and Philip Johnson's Glass House. The bamboo façade and metal frame are a reminder of Pierre Chareau's Maison de verre. Koolhaas added his own signature to these echoes with a roof pool and sloping posts like fragile reeds.

Toyo Ito ▼

1941, Seoul (Korea)

Sendai Multimedia Library, Japan, 1996

Architectural model at 1:100
Plastic, 42.8 x 117.9 x 78.9 cm
Purchased in 2001
AM 2001-2-23

Philippe Starck ▲

1949, Paris (France)

Sunflower, 1991

Pivoting street lamp
Cast iron, optics; 900 cm
Gift of Jean-Claude Decaux, 1992
AM 1993-1-408

A star in the global design firmament, Philippe Starck harnesses, reinterprets, relocates and transforms the archetypes of our hyperconsumer society.

This street lamp, commissioned by a company making street furniture, is articulated to follow the light, in the manner of a sunflower, its beam being directed at the road at night in order to guide cars. In the morning, nothing is left of this organic source of light, half lobster's claw, half ear of corn, except a slender pointed mast, blending into the countryside.

Born in Seoul but resident in Japan, Toyo Ito tends to blur the borders between interior and exterior in his architecture. He uses technology to create a sense of lightness, even immateriality in his buildings. Thus, this Sendai multimedia library in Japan appears to blend into the landscape, the structure seemingly welcoming light and the whole environment into itself. Over and above the transparency of the façades, the modulation of the decks of different storeys enables the interchange between people and means of communication to be improved, while the minimalism of the load-bearing columns (resembling trees) allows the flow of people between different sectors of the library to be seen. Its users are, according to Ito, "a flow of electrons in a body linked to nature."

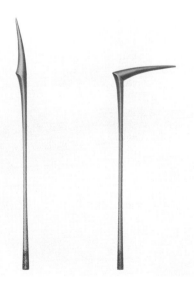

Ron Arad

1951, Tel Aviv (Israel)

Rolling Volume chair,
1991

Polished stainless steel
80 x 85 x 95; 70 kg
Purchased in 1992
AM 1992-1-291

Executed in stainless
steel, this rocking
chair constitutes
a single volume.
With its rounded
shape, it tilts back-
wards and forwards
despite its con-
siderable weight
(154 lbs). Manu-
factured as a limited
edition, it was the
result of research
work carried out
by Israeli designer Ron Arad for
his Big Easy Collection in 1988.
The shape and polished welds

create lines apparently drawn
freehand, contrasting with the steel
and weight of the object.

Patrick Tosani

1954, Boissy-l'Aillerie (France)

Mask no. 6, 1998
Cibachrome print, 113 × 140 cm
Purchased in 2000
AM 2000-24

In his photographs, Patrick Tosani (an architect by training) focuses on questions of scale, monumentality and the relationship between interior and exterior. Several of his series play with the volume and form of an ideal architecture, whether it concerns the presentation of the soles of shoes, chewed nails or garments discarded like empty envelopes.

Masks is a series of photographs of starched trousers that have retained the imprint of the body, the photo being taken from above. Instead of a garment, the image of a mask appears, the envelope of the face, indicating the absence of the body.

► Marc Newson

1963, Sydney (Australia)

Alufelt Chair, 1993
Polished aluminium. Inside surface painted
85 × 67 × 100 cm
Purchased in 2001
AM 2001-1-153

Marc Newson is one of the most remarkable designers of his generation, sought after by producers of objects since the early 1990s. Formerly a student of jewellery, he is fascinated by the alliance of textures and materials, and makes use of his discoveries in his biomorphic creations. The *Alufelt Chair* is part of a collection of furniture including a table and armchair. This chair, more sculptural than solid, invites the body to sink into it, the back tightening to the level of the sitter, the curve of the surround being shaped to the dimensions of the human back. Its flexible, dual-colour look and petal-shaped front legs also form an orchid, its maw open and its corolla open to the sky and the earth.

Andreas Gursky

1955, Leipzig (former East Germany)

99 c, 1999
Cibachrome print, 220 x 420 cm
Purchased in 2000
AM 2000-96

German artist Andreas Gursky photographs people caught in the trap of their own excess. Lost in the anthill of the Chicago stock market, the storeys of a bank skyscraper in Hongkong or the Olympic Games at Albertville, the viewer gets lost in these images that are static and yet encroaching and dizzying. Here, in the shelves of a multicoloured discount store, it is the sheer mass of products, their promiscuity, variety and – despite this – uniformity that constitute the attraction and the source of alarm. It is a coloured universe you think you can never revel in and which already disgusts us. Humans are everywhere but almost indiscernible, and dominated by the world they have created.

Pierre Huyghe

1962, Antony (France)

The Third Memory, 1999

3 videotapes, colour, stereo soundtrack (English),
14 numerical prints (60 x 80 cm); 2 rooms
Co-production purchase
Anna Sanders Films, 1999
AM 1999-154

The Third Memory is an installation by
Pierre Huyghe that explores memory
between media, fiction and reality. The
artist assembles in it press cuttings and
a filmed document relating to a hold-up
that took place in Brooklyn in 1972, and
which Sydney Lumet used as the basis
for his film *Dog Day Afternoon*. In the first
room, we get one of the newspapers and
a broadcast of the time. In the second, we
get a double projection made by Huyghe,
which shows the real protagonist replay-
ing the hold-up, according to his version
of the facts, disputing the scenes inserted
from Lumet's film but also filling in the
obvious gaps in his memory.

IRCAM
Sounds, Musical or Otherwise

✦ In a separate building, opposite the fountain in Place Igor-Stravinsky

Music just had to be included in a National Centre of Art and Culture. That is why Georges Pompidou decided to create IRCAM in 1969 as a non-profit-making organisation combining scientific research with music and acoustics. The new organisation was directed by composer and conductor Pierre Boulez. From that moment, IRCAM became – as it has remained – a unique organisation. It carries out research and development work in disciplines such as IT, physics and acoustics applied to musical creation.

Machinations, *Georges Aperghis*,
June 2000

History

Its objectives

Alongside this research function, IRCAM invites a large number of composers to its studios every year, resulting in the creation of 20 to 25 works linking classical performers with new technologies. It also provides several educational programmes restricted to professionals (various degree courses and a doctoral course) or alternatively open to a broad public (conferences and debates). Finally, it provides access to a multimedia library with a substantial and constantly growing collection on post-war music. The books, records, videos, websites and even scores – all available for consultation on the spot or online – constitute a valuable and efficient source of information.

A specific activity

However, IRCAM remains the least-known part of the Centre, primarily because it is not contained within the Centre. When it was set up, it was entirely subterranean, situated beneath the fountain in Place Igor-Stravinsky, between the Centre and Saint-Merri church. Today, it occupies neighbouring buildings as well, with a red brick tower designed in 1996 by Renzo Piano standing at the corner, to make the institution more visible.

An important part of IRCAM's activities is in specialised and scientific sectors. In fact, the Institute uses its skills to develop software to enrich composers' writing and set up international exchanges with major universities or centres of research. Otherwise, partnerships are developed with the industrial world to work on acoustic research, particularly in the field of telecommunications and motor transport.

Opening up to the public

However, it is via its specialist research that IRCAM has helped to popularise musical creation on computer and to expand the scope of the ubiquitous electronic music found today. Its intention is to become increasingly accessible to every kind of public. With this in mind, it facilitates visits to the Institute, conferences and debates, personal and online access to the multimedia library, and also musical seasons presenting the compositions created within its

Activities

• Concerts and performances (musical season with the Ensemble Intercontemporain and Agora Festival).
• Meetings, conferences, symposia:
– commentated workshop concerts
– series of theme-based conferences: music and dance, music and text, music and perception, music and space;
– symposia.
• Musical IT workshops for adults and children.
• Courses aimed at different publics depending on the themes and technical skills required.
• Extended courses: musical IT composition degree course and training (selection by a reading panel), DEA Atiam (Diploma in Acoustics, Signal Processing and IT Applied to Music).
• Multimedia library: 15,000 books and periodicals and more than 8,000 scores, 2,500 recordings from concerts, videos and music CD-ROMs. Consultable online on www.ircam.fr.
• Forum: distribution of IRCAM musical IT software programmes.

An anecdote

Problem: electric cars don't make any noise. You wouldn't hear them coming down the street … IRCAM is carrying out advisory work for motor manufacturers in order to create the noise of an electric car.

The Agora Festival

A two-week event in June, the festival combines and juxtaposes musical, choreographic and theatrical creations. The concerts and performances are presented in various halls in Paris and the Paris region, particularly those of the Pompidou Centre (as co-productions with the Spectacles Vivants section of the DDC). Its ever-growing success shows how much the public expects artists to build bridges between disciplines so their works respond to each other and open up new fields of creation.

Strumentale,
Olga de Soto

*Forum
workshop*

*The outside of
the building*

walls, organised in Paris and on tour with the Ensemble Intercontemporain or numerous other bodies abroad. The largest of these tours was when Boulez's *Répons* [Response] was presented across the USA in 1986, in Moscow and Leningrad in 1990, and in Tokyo in 1995. IRCAM is equally associated with productions of sung works in Salzburg, Brussels and even the Opéra in Paris.

Moreover, since 1998, IRCAM has organised its own festival, Agora, which links musical creation with other artistic disciplines (dance, theatre or cinema). It is in this same spirit of multidisciplinary development that IRCAM set up a new department of choreographic creation in 1999.

IRCAM has thus proved unique of its kind as a tool, putting basic research at the service of musical creation.

Further reading

IRCAM distributes its creations in the form of books and periodicals, CDs and CD-ROMs:

- Books

Lire l'Ircam, 1996, special edition by *Cahiers de l'Ircam*, published to mark the inauguration of new study buildings and the mediatheque, 184 p., € 30,49
L'Écoute, collected texts by Peter Szendy, 2000, co-published by Ircam-Centre Pompidou/l'Harmattan, 320 p., € 24,30

- CDs

Ircam, les années 90, 1998, triple CD with an audio presentation (in French) of the Institute's activities and extracts of musical works created at IRCAM, € 15.24

- CD-ROMs
A Visit to Ircam, 1997, in French and English with an animated presentation of IRCAM's activities, € 22.87
[a set of listening games in French]

🖥 www.ircam.fr

The IRCAM site comprises a very detailed presentation of the Institute (organisation, objectives, output, online boutique, etc.), access to the catalogue and part of the multimedia library collection.

IRCAM software

The programmes are original, very powerful and more or less specialised products, with no commercial equivalents. The programmes include:
- Audiosculpt, allowing a sound to be modified visually;
- Diphone Studio, dedicated to sound morphing;
- Modalys, used to create virtual instruments.
All three products as a package cost € 275 (individual purchase). They are available online (www.ircam.fr/forum), by email (admin-forum@ircam.fr), by post addressed to IRCAM (Ircam, Relations extérieures, 1 pl. Igor-Stravinsky, 75004 Paris) or directly from reception at the Institute.

ℹ

- Address:
1, place Igor-Stravinsky, 75004 Paris

- Opening hours
Reception and sales of IRCAM books, periodicals, discs and CD-ROMS: Mondays to Fridays 10 am – 6 pm

- Telephone enquiries
– IRCAM: 01- 44 78 48 43
– Multimedia library: 01- 44 78 47 44

- Website: www.ircam.fr.

Discover the rich variety of the collections at the National Museum of Modern Art/Centre Georges Pompidou

**La collection
de design du Centre
Georges Pompidou**
210 pages. 22 x 28 cm.
with CD-ROM.
€ 39,64

**La collection
du Musée national
d'art moderne II,
1986/1996**
380 pages. 23,5 x 30 cm.
€ 60,98

**La collection
d'architecture du Centre
Georges Pompidou.
Projets d'architecture,
1906/1998**
376 pages. 23,5 x 30 cm.
€ 60,22

**La collection
cinématographique
du Musée national
d'art moderne.
L'art du mouvement**
496 pages. 23,5 x 30 cm.
€ 68,60

**Une histoire
matérielle
XXe/Mnam/Collections**
872 pages. 19 x 22,8 cm.
French/English
€ 39,64

**Antoine Pevsner
dans les collections
du Mnam**
112 pages. 22 x 28 cm.
€ 27,44

**Marcel Duchamp
dans les collections
du Mnam**
160 pages. 22 x 28 cm.
€ 28,97

**L'atelier Brancusi.
La collection**
288 pages. 23,5 x 30 cm.
€ 42,69

You'll find a complete
and up-to-date list
of publications
on our website:
www.centrepompidou.fr

Centre
Pompidou

Your visit to the Centre Pompidou

You can spare two hours

This is the minimum time you need to profit from a visit to some of the Centre's facilities. But make no mistake, the Pompidou Centre is a large entity that deserves a lot more than 120 minutes of your attention!

Here's the menu (each item about 2 hours). You can:

- visit the National Museum of Modern Art on your own or with a lecturer (see *A to Z of Practical Information*), before relaxing a while on the Museum terraces;
- look round the temporary exhibition on Level 1 (South Gallery);
- visit the temporary exhibition on Level 6, afterwards taking in the panoramic view of Paris to south, west or north;
- see what IRCAM is about (Thursday mornings by appointment);
- explore the BPI (Public Reference Library), or even sit down there and do that spot of research you always said you would do one day;
- join a Sunday 'Active Visit to the Museum' *en famille* (for adults and children of 5+);
- depending on the day, sit in on a 'Collège du Centre' conference (Grande Salle, Level –1 and Screen 1, Level 1) or join a 'One Sunday, One Work' session, (Petite Salle, Level –1);
- depending on the programme, watch a film or an evening performance.

You have a free afternoon

You can now take the time for a programme taking in different activities

Menu 1:
the whole works!
- free visit to the 'Crossroads of Creation'
- Museum or exhibition
- BPI
- IRCAM (Thursday mornings)

Menu 2:
the Museum and exhibitions
- Museum,
- exhibitions,
- Brancusi Studio,
- Children's Gallery.

⚠ *There is a special ticket (Un jour au centre/A Day at the Centre) for this menu.*

Menu 3:
a studious afternoon at BPI, exploring, researching, studying, listening to discs or watching films, etc.

- the mezzanine café (Forum, Level 1) or kiosk cafeteria (BPI, Level 2), for a coffee or sandwich
- relaxation and shopping (bookshop and Design Boutique);
- a visit to the Museum's collections (Levels 4 and 5);
- depending on the programme, a performance (concert, dance, etc.) on Level –1 of the Forum or a film (Level 1 or –1);
- dinner (or lunch) in Georges, the restaurant on Level 6 with a panoramic terrace.

Menu 4:
studying and shopping
- a conference or film, depending on the programme,
- purchases in the bookshop and/or Design Boutique.
- You can still fit in a little something, so why not drop in on the temporary exhibition on Level 1 (South Gallery)? It's generally smaller than the one on Level 6. Alternatively, browse through some books at the BPI.

You've got a whole day

Go back to all the activities in the **Two Hours** section above and select a few of these to make a programme to suit you. But make sure your visit to the Centre doesn't turn into a marathon. Get a taste for it, and you'll be back!

A typical day might take in:
- a visit to IRCAM
- exploring the Library (BPI)
- an exhibition on Level 1 or Level 6

⚠ *If you have children, think of activities specially designed for them – the educational workshop or exploration of the Museum in the Children's Gallery (Wednesdays and Saturdays).*

You're unable to come to the Centre

- Our website, www.centrepompidou.fr, provides a virtual exploration of the Museum's collections and an opportunity to consult the BPI (Library) and IRCAM catalogues.
- A CD-ROM, *La Collection du Centre Georges Pompidou*, published by the Pompidou Centre/Infogrames, Paris, 1997, is a virtual presentation (in French) of works in the National Museum of Modern Art (MNAM).

From A to Z
Practical information of the Centre Pompidou

Entry via the plaza, Place Georges Pompidou, 100 yards from Boulevard Sébastopol.

Metro
metro stations Rambuteau (Line 11), Hôtel de Ville (Lines 1 and 11), Châtelet (Lines 1, 4, 11 and 14) RER station Châtelet/Les Halles (Lines A, B and D)

Buses
buses 21, 29, 38, 47, 58, 69, 70, 72, 74, 75, 76, 81, 85, 96

Parking
parking access under ground via Les Halles or Rue Beaubourg (corner of Rue Rambuteau)

Annual pass (Laissez-passer)
- A 12-month season ticket (starting any date) entitling the holder to free entry at any time to the Museum, exhibitions and cinemas (except during festivals), reduced prices for performance events and numerous other benefits.
- Priority entry at the main entrance, Place Georges-Pompidou.
- Bi-monthly programme sent to home address
- Different methods of charging possible.
- Information and sales:
  – Laissez-passer area, Level 0, 1 pm – 7 pm, except Tuesdays, 1 May and public holidays;
  – by phone on 01-44 78 **14 63**, Mondays to Fridays, 9 am – 6 pm.

Audioguides
- Exhibitions: available in French, English and Italian at certain exhibitions. Available at the entrance to exhibitions.

- Museum: available in French, English, Italian, German and Spanish, at the entrance to the Museum.

Bookshops
- In the Forum, Level 0 (r. h. side).
- In the Museum, Level 4.
- Level 6, major exhibitions floor.

BPI – see **Libraries**.

Brochures and programmes
These provide detailed information about the Pompidou Centre's programmes. Available from Enquiries (Forum, Level 0) and, depending on their speciality, at the BPI, Museum or IRCAM reception desks.

Cafés and restaurant
- mezzanine café, Forum, Level 1
- le kiosque cafeteria, Library, Level 2
- Georges Restaurant, with panoramic terrace, Level 6, reservations on 01-44 78 **47 99** (entry from outside, Place Georges-Pompidou, separate lift).

Cash machines
In the Forum, Level 0

Children
- Children's Gallery:
  – exhibition daily except

Tuesdays, 11.30 am – 2 pm and 4 – 7 pm. Free to under 18s, or holders of annual passes or Museum tickets.
  – workshops (6 – 12-year-olds) Wednesdays, Saturdays and during school holidays; family day Sundays (for adults and children 5+).
- specific activities:
  – 'From the Workshop to the Museum' (for 6 – 12-year-olds) – over three Wednesdays or a single Saturday session
  – 'Dance and Visual Arts' workshops (for 6 – 12-year-olds) and 'Visual Arts and Technologies' (for 9 – 12-year-olds) – over three Wednesdays.
  – 'Active Visits to the Museum' (for 6 –12-year-olds) – Wednesdays; family sessions Sundays (for adults and children 5+).
- enrolment and reservations:
  – individual visitors, enrolment for all workshops and 'Active Visits to the Museum' – daily except Tuesdays and Sundays on 01-44 78 **49 13**;
  – school groups, registration compulsory for visits to the Centre, the Museum and exhibitions with speaker or presenter:
  – colleges and lycées: visits to the Museum: 01-44 78 **40 54**;

The escalator at night (detail)

Self-study area in the BPI library (detail)

IRCAM Forum workshop (detail)

visits to exhibitions and the Centre: 01-44 78 **12 57**.
– nursery schools and leisure centres: visits to the Centre / the Museum: 01-44 78 **49 17**; visits to exhibitions: 01-44 78 **12 57**.
• IRCAM: musical IT workshops for schoolchildren, enrolment on 01-44 78 **48 23**.
⚠ *Programmes and charges are in the Centre's brochures or online on www.centrepompidou.fr. Priority access from Place Georges-Pompidou via the line marked Visites commentées/Conférences.*

Cinemas
• in the Forum: Screen 2, Level –1 (150 seats, entry – see **Live performances**)
– Screen 1, Level 1 (320 seats, entry – see **Libraries**)
• documentary film, Wednesdays at 12.30 pm and 8 pm.
• film for children, Wednesdays at 2.30 pm.
⚠ *Information about programmes on 01-44 78 44 49 and online www.bpi.fr.*
*- documentary film festival – see **Festivals**.*

Cloakroom
In the Forum, Level 0.

Concerts and performances
• in the Forum, Level –1:
– Grand Salle (440 seats, dance, theatre, music),
– Petite Salle (160 places, conferences),
– IRCAM, Place Igor-Stravinsky.

Conferences
• Spoken Reviews – themed surveys of various creative fields.
• social forums, focusing on current cultural developments, audiovisuals and

new media, or relating to exhibitions in the Centre's programme.
• 'Collège du Centre', Grand Salle, Level – 1, and Screen 1, Level 1. Check charges. Free with annual pass.
• 'One Sunday, One Work' (for adults): Petite Salle. Level –1. Check charges. Free with annual pass.
• Museum:
– 'Looking at the Works' – series exploring individual aspects of 20th-century creation, based on the Museum collection;
– 'Museum Rendezvous' – an original, theme-based series looking in depth at the collections in the Museum (Mondays and Fridays);
– 'Meeting …': a regular series of encounters where creative artists come to the Museum or exhibition to meet the public and talk about their work.
⚠ *Programmes and charges in the Centre's brochures or website www.centrepompidou.fr. Priority access from Place Georges-Pompidou via the line marked Visites commentées/Conférences.*
• BPI (Library): symposia of international scope on themes to do with writings and books;
• IRCAM: symposia and series of theme-based conferences (e.g. music and dance, music and perception, music and space).

Courses
• IRCAM provides:
– training for different publics depending on the topics and skills required;
– extended courses: from training to degree courses in composition and

musical IT (selection by a reading panel), DEA Atiam (Diploma in Acoustics, Signal Processing and IT Applied to Music);
– Contact: IRCAM, Service Pédagogie, 1 Place Igor-Stravinsky, 75004 Paris, tel. 01-44 78 **48 23**, fax: 01-44 78 **15 60**, info-pedagogique@ircam.fr.
• The DAEP provides:
– training courses for teachers, librarians and staff of the educational service;
– supplementary training in the regions and abroad;
– contact: DAEP, Service de l'Action Éducative, 75191 Paris Cedex 04, or tel. 01-44 78 **43 16** (Mondays and Tuesdays), fax: 01-44 78 **13 04**.

Design Boutique
Entry free, from the Forum, Level 1 (via escalator on the left, stairs or lift at the back of the Forum behind the pit). Collections of designer articles, including some represented in the Centre's collections.

Disabled visitors
• Reception of the blind and those with motor disabilities, information on 01-44 78 **49 54**. Entry

Day ticket to the Centre

Cinema sign in the Forum

The colours of the Centre

via Rue du Renard, corner of Rue Saint-Merri. Parking spaces reserved on Levels −2 and −3 of the pay car park (entry from Rue Rambuteau and Rue des Halles). Exit the top of Place Georges-Pompidou.
- Multimedia information terminal, touch, visual and sound modes (Forum, Level 0), explaining the organisation of the Centre and giving information about activities.
- Visitors with motor disabilities or impaired mobility: all the activities and programmed events on the Centre's premises are accessible.
- Exploration visits to the Centre for those with impaired sight or hearing: Saturdays, bookings via 01-44 78 **49 54** or handicap@cnac-gp.fr, also for the deaf: fax 01-44 78 **16 73**, Minitel dialogue 01-44 78 **14 37**.
- Museum: visits in sign language for the deaf, tactile presentation or oral visit for the blind and partially sighted, presentations in the collections for mentally handicapped visitors. - Information and booking on 01-44 78 **49 54**, or handicap@cnac-gp.fr. For the deaf: fax 01-44 78 **16 73**, Minitel dialogue 01-44 78 **14 37**.
- BPI: blind and partially sighted – contact the BPI reception or 01-44 78 **12 75**. Volunteers (by appointment) and specially adapted materials are available for reading and assisting research.

Enquiries and information, Pompidou Centre
- General information: in the Forum, Level 0 (various brochures available).

- Museum, Level 4.
- BPI (Library), Level 1 of the Library, or contactable externally through the rapid information service, by post (BPI-Info – 75197 Paris, Cedex 04), email (bpi-info@bpi.fr) or fax (01-44 78 **45 10**).
- IRCAM reception desk, Place Igor-Stravinsky.
- Performances and live events: general information desk, Forum, Level 0.

Exhibitions
- Level 1, right-hand side of mezzanine – South Gallery.
- Level −1, in the foyer (short exhibitions often relating to the live events programme).
- Level 4: Museum gallery (temporary exhibitions highlighting the Museum's acquisitions policy, paying tribute to donors or interpreting a group of works) and graphic art gallery.
- Level 6: Gallery 1 and Gallery 2.

Festivals
- Agora – two-week event in June. Combines musical, choreographic and theatrical works.
- Documentary Film Festival – takes place in spring, entirely devoted to documentary films.
- Videodance – an annual festival giving the public a chance to see exceptional archive films and explore choreographed creations conceived specifically for video.

⚠ *Programme details of every festival are shown in the Centre's leaflets and online at www.centrepompidou.fr.*

Films
(see Cinemas and Festivals)

Getting around in the Centre
- Which entrance should I use?
- Generally there is only one main entrance, from the plaza, Place Georges-Pompidou.
- A second entrance on Rue du Renard is exclusively for the use of Library readers and is open on weekends, public holidays and when Vigipirate anti-terrorist measures are in force.
- What leads where from the Forum?
- escalator on the left mezzanine (Level 1) and flights of escalators (*chénille*) leading to upper levels, Design Boutique, BPI (Library) and Screen 1;
- escalator on the right mezzanine (Level 1), café and South Gallery exhibition;
- escalators at the back, behind the pit mezzanine (Level 1), BPI (Library), Screen 1 and Design Boutique;
- stairs beside the pit Level −1 (foyer, Grand Salle, Petite Salle, studio);
- lifts at the back, behind the pit mezzanine and Level −1;
- Where do the *chénille* (flight of escalators) and lifts at the front of the Centre lead (available only to visitors with a Museum or exhibition ticket)?
- Museum Documentation department (Level 3);
- MNAM-CCI (National Museum of Modern Art / Industrial Design Centre);
- Level 6 (exhibitions, panorama, Georges Restaurant.

Groups (10 + people, reservations compulsory)
- BPI (Library) – groups of visitors welcome a.m. Bookings: 01-44 78 **43 45**.

- reservations for the Museum:
  – visits with accompanying Pompidou Centre lecturer, tel. 01-44 78 **40 54**;
  – unaccompanied visits, tel. 01-44 78 **42 11**.
- reservations for exhibitions:
  – visits with accompanying Pompidou Centre lecturer, tel. 01-44 78 **12 57**;
  – unaccompanied visits, tel. 01-44 78 **46 25**.

Guided visits
(see also **Conferences**)
- BPI (Library): literary walks round areas of Paris that have inspired writers. Information on 01-44 78 **44 49**, online at www.bpi.fr.
- Exhibitions:
  – regular guided visits (general public), please consult Enquiries, the Pompidou Centre website or brochures;
  – groups by reservation on 01-44 78 **12 57**.
- IRCAM – visits Thursday mornings by appointment, bookings on 01-44 78 **48 43**.
- MNAM (National Museum of Modern Art) – regular guided visits (general public), groups by booking on 01-44 78 **40 54**. Programme and charges in the Centre's bimonthly programme or its website (www.centre-pompidou.fr).
- 'Promenades urbaines (City Walks),' Saturdays or Sundays, accompanied by architects or academics. Booking compulsory, via the Institut français d'architecture, on 01-**46 33 84 41**.

Information
See **Enquiries**.

Internet
See **Websites**.

IRCAM
(institute specialising in computer-based music and acoustics) Located outside the Centre, on the left, after you return to the Place Georges-Pompidou, besides the Jean Tinguely/Niki de Saint-Phalle fountain in Place Igor-Stravinsky.

Libraries
- BPI (Public Reference Library), Level 1 in the Forum, mezzanine level, l. h. side.
- Documentation, National Museum of Modern Art, MNAM (Level 3) presents an account of 20th-century artistic creation in the visual arts, design, architecture, experimental cinema, photography and video.
- IRCAM multimedia library (Place Igor-Stravinsky): 15,000 books and periodicals and more than 8,000 scores, 2,500 recordings of concerts, videos and music CD-ROMS. Online consultation at www.ircam.fr.

Opening hours
- Daily (except Tuesdays and 1 May), 11 am – 10 pm.
- Museum and exhibitions: 11 am–9 pm, last entry 8 pm, galleries close at 8.45 pm.
- Major exhibitions on Level 6: same hours as the Museum, plus Thursday evenings to 11 pm (last entry 10 pm).
- Brancusi Studio: 1 – 7 pm
- BPI (Library): 12 noon – 10 pm weekdays, 11 am – 10 pm Saturdays, Sundays and public holidays.
- IRCAM: visits Thursdays by appointment.

Post office
In the Forum, Level 0.

Telephone enquiries
(**01-44 78**-…)
- General: 01-44 78 **12 33**. Answering service on same number: after 7.30 pm and on Sundays/public holidays.
- Disabled enquirers: 01-44 78 **49 54**; handicap@cnac-gp.fr; deaf enquirers, Minitel dialogue: 01-44 78 **14 37**.
- BPI (Library): phone enquiries on 01-44 78 **12 75**, 10 am – 10 pm weekdays (except Tuesday) and 11 am – 10 pm weekends.
- IRCAM: 01-44 78 **48 43**; multimedia library: 01-44 78 **47 44**.

Telephones
- Forum, Level 0
- BPI, in the kiosk, Level 2
- Museum entrance, Level 4
- Level 6, beside the bookshop

Tickets and charges
- Ticket office in the Forum, Level 0.
- Ticket machines (only full rate tickets, payment by banker's card) in the Forum, Level 0, and on Level 6.
- Un jour au Centre ticket – access the same day to all exhibitions, the Museum, the Brancusi Studio and Children's Gallery.
- National Museum of Modern Art/Brancusi Studio – the ticket also allows entry to the Children's Gallery, but not to temporary exhibitions.
- Exhibitions:
  – charges vary according to exhibition. Enquire at the ticket desk (*Caisse*).
  – tickets also allow entry to the Museum, Brancusi Studio and Children's Gallery.

Children's workshop, based on Dubuffet

IRCAM building seen from the fountain in Place Stravinsky

Open Day at IRCAM

*Guided tour
for the blind*

- Debates and conferences are mostly free-of-charge.
- Reduced-rate tickets: ask at Enquiries, Forum, Level 0.
- Free entry:
  – Forum and Library;
  – Museum (under 18s, annual pass holders, jobseekers and, on first Sunday of each month, the general public);
  – exhibitions (under 13s, annual pass holders and jobseekers).
- Films and live events: ask at Enquiries, Forum, Level 0
  – Tickets for performances are on sale at the Centre's ticket office 14 days in advance.
  – Reservations and sale of tickets for certain performances and exhibitions available 30 days in advance at www.fnac.com, in FNAC and Carrefour stores and via the France-Billet network (events: **0892-683 622**, exhibitions: **0892 684 694**).

⚠ *Entry to the panoramic viewpoint (Level 6) only on presentation of a valid ticket to the Museum or exhibitions.*

Toilets
- Forum, Level 0.
- BPI (Public Reference Library), Level 2.
- Museum, Levels 4 and 5.
- On Level 6.

Websites
1) www.centrepompidou.fr
   Set up in 1995, the Pompidou Centre's website

was completely redesigned during the renovation works.
- *Agenda* covers the current news of the Centre's programme and activities.
- You can subscribe for a newsletter about the activities.
- *Événements* (Events) gives information about all the specific activities at the Centre.
- *Expositions* contains summaries of the various exhibitions, with images.
- *The Musée* (Museum) section deals with the displays and new acquisitions and provides a chronicle of 20th-century art for educational purposes.
- *Netart* provides virtual exhibitions of works conceived for Internet and commissions set up in collaboration with international institutions.
- The *Documentation* part is intended for research, and includes exhibition catalogues, archive collections, etc.
- *Éditions* is the publication department's online catalogue of publications.
2) www.newmedia-arts.org
   Accesses the New Media Encyclopaedia, the first catalogue of new media on a European scale, in French, English and German.
3) www.bpi.fr
   The BPI (Library) website comprises the Library catalogue and a large number

of tools and services (see chapter on the Library at the front).
4) www.ircam.fr
   The IRCAM site provides a very detailed presentation of the Institute (organisation, objectives, output, online boutique, etc.) and access to a catalogue and part of the multimedia library collection.

Workshops
(see also **Children**)
- IRCAM:
  – musical IT workshops for adults,
  – commentated workshop-concerts.
- BPI (Library):
  familiarisation sessions for research tools,
  – meetings, debates, reading workshops (series).

Zoom
to those phone numbers. All phone numbers in this section except France-Billet (**Tickets**) and the Institut français d'architecture (**Guided visits**) begin with **01-44 78**. Only the last four digits of each number vary. From abroad, dial **+33 1-44 78**...

Index of Artists

Photographic credits

Photos CNAC/MNAM
    Distribution RMN, Paris.
    Photographers : Jacque-
    line Hyde, Jacques
    Faujour, Georges
    Méguerditchian, Jean-
    Claude Planchet, Adam
    Rzepka : pp. 34-144.
Documentation Centre
    Pompidou, Paris.
    Photos G. Méguerdit-
    chian, front and back
    covers and pp. 4, 6, 9, 10
    (middle), 11, 14, 17 (top),
    19 (top), 20, 22, 28, 30, 32,
    152-3, 154, 156 (left).
Documentation Centre
    Pompidou, Paris.

Photo Bernard Vincent,
    p. 10 (top).
Photo Nicolas Borel, Paris,
    p. 10 (bottom).
Photo D. R., p. 17 (bottom).
    All rights reserved.
Documentation DAEP.
    Centre Georges Pompi-
    dou, Paris. Photos Élisa-
    beth Amzallag-Augé, pp.
    19 (middle), 19 (bottom).
Photothèque BPI. Centre
    Georges Pompidou, Paris.
    pp. 24, 26, 155 (left).
Ircam. Centre Pompidou,
    Paris. Photos Nabil
    Boutros, pp. 146/7, 149
    (middle), 155 (right).

Documentation Centre
    Pompidou, Paris.
    Photo Jean-Claude
    Planchet, p. 149 (top).
Ircam. Centre Pompidou,
    Paris. Photo Myr
    Muratet, pp. 149 (bottom),
    157 (right).
Documentation DAEP.
    Centre Georges Pom-
    pidou, Paris. Photo
    Max-Henri de Larminat,
    p. 157 (left).
Ircam. Centre Pompidou,
    Paris. Photo Jacques
    Dufour, p. 158 (left).
Photo Georges Coupigny,
    Paris, p. 158 (right).